Chopper!

Chopper!

The Illustrated Story of Helicopters in Action

by BERN KEATING

RAND McNALLY & COMPANY
Chicago • New York • San Francisco

Quotations by Igor Sikorsky from Igor Sikorsky:
His Three Careers in Aviation, *by Frank J.
Delear, copyright © 1969 by Frank J. Delear,
reprinted courtesy of Dodd, Mead &
Company, publisher.*

Library of Congress Cataloging in Publication Data

Keating, Bern.
    CHOPPER: THE ILLUSTRATED STORY OF HELICOPTERS IN ACTION.
    Includes index.
    1. Helicopters.   2. Search and Rescue Operations.
I. Title.
TL716.K37   629.133'35   76-21815
ISBN 0-528-81842-2

First printing, 1976

Acknowledgments

The author is forever amazed by the generosity of the helicopter folk who gave up formidable slices of their busy lives and trusted invaluable photographs, memorabilia, and rare volumes to my care with no hope of profit.

With the uneasy certainty that, as usual, I am overlooking the one person who helped me more than all the others put together, I wish to thank the following: Weston B. Haskell, Jr., of Kaman Corporation; Dick Tipton of Bell Helicopters; Dick Tierney of Fort Rucker, Alabama; Jim Bixler and Bill Baker of Petroleum Helicopters; Harry Lounsbury of the American Helicopter Society; Tom MacNew of Boeing Vertol; Frank J. Delear of Sikorsky; H. Frank Gregory, now a retired brigadier general living in Tulsa, Oklahoma; Jean Ross Howard, the Whirly-Girl from Washington, D.C.; John M. Slattery, now a retired lieutenant colonel living in Oxon Hill, Maryland; and the officers and noncommissioned officers of the various historical sections of the armed services.

Special mention must be made of the courtesies shown by Norman Lornie and John Lampl of British Airways and the brilliant interview granted by Jock Cameron, a distinguished pioneer of British rotary-wing aviation and chief of British Airways' helicopter operations.

Contents

Foreword

As these words are being written, repeated earthquake shocks are ravaging Guatemala. The most urgent plea from distressed officials on the scene is for helicopters and more helicopters. And, as usual, they are swarming in from all directions.

There is something special about the machines that excites a peculiar kind of behavior from their passengers, and even more so from their pilots, inspiring them beyond the normal workaday level of performance. It may have something to do with the rhythm of the rotors, a rhythm closely matching the heartbeat, that has gained them the name of "choppers." The first lift-off, when the pilot hovers for a moment to be sure everything is working right and then swoops off, invariably speeds the pulse with excitement.

So when the call goes out for help, as it is now going out from Guatemala, helicopter people perform prodigies—exhibiting courage, devotion to their human duties, and endurance far beyond what could be expected.

My first encounter with the machines was early in their history when I rode some of the first Bell helicopters to the earliest rigs in the Gulf of Mexico. During the short-lived and lamented operation of Sabena's helicopter network linking Western European cities, I flew from Paris to Brussels in a Sikorsky S-58, skimming over the north French and Belgian countryside low enough to wave at peasants tilling their fields, to peer into the courtyards of chateaux, and to admire the tidy gardens of the Flemish bourgeoisie.

Later, I traveled to the remote corners of Bangladesh (then East Pakistan) in a Pakistan Air Lines S-61, seeing from my low-altitude vantage point the peculiar relationship of the Bengali people with their rivers. From the deck of the helicopter the fragile hold the people have on their tillable land, forever threatened by disastrous floods, is evident in a way impossible to see from ground level. And the Sikorsky set me down in distant villages where no fixed-wing plane will ever land because there is not enough solid earth to form a continuous runway.

Years later, I flew in the very same machine, sold by Pakistan to British Airways, to an oil rig 100 miles from Aberdeen, Scotland, in the North Sea. A worker had fallen from a rig and drowned. His replacement, like all the crew, arrived by air. Because the rig had a dangerous projection, the pilot backed his machine aboard, guiding himself with a boom attached below the platform for a reference point.

To get to the Isles of Scilly, those semitropical rocks that are all that remain of the legendary Arthurian land of Lyonesse, now submerged by the sea, you have two choices: a four- to six-hour ride in stormy seas aboard a freighter or a 20-minute lark across the Cornish countryside and the whitecaps of the Atlantic in a smooth-riding helicopter, piloted by a chap who quite cheerfully loops about the archipelago to give you a view of the bird-swarming flower beds of that improbable little paradise.

The astonishing thing is that some travelers actually take the ship.

BERN KEATING

Chopper!

1

In the Beginning

I say that this instrument made by a helix [Greek for "spiral" or "screw"] and well made, that is to say of flaxen linen of which one has closed the pores with starch, and is turned with a great speed, the said helix is able to make a screw in the air and to climb high.

—Leonardo da Vinci

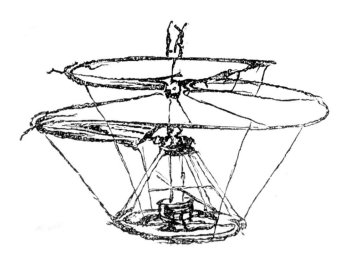

This sketch, made by Leonardo da Vinci about 1483, has been hailed as the first helicopter design. Unfortunately, aeronautical engineers say that the device is unflyable. The Renaissance genius was not the first on the field anyhow. The principle of using resistance to air to generate power was first discovered by whoever first rigged a sail on a ship or flew a kite. Back in the thirteenth century, Roger Bacon theorized on the possibilities of mechanical flight by using air resistance. Leonardo da Vinci may have been the first to suggest using an airscrew for lift-off.

It is almost a federal law that books about helicopters must credit Leonardo da Vinci with designing the first vertical-flight machine—though it never flew and, according to aeronautical engineers who have studied the replicas based on his design, is not likely to. Still, Leonardo's sketches and monographs showed he had some understanding of the rotor principle, verified by demonstrations of present-day models.

Actually, Neanderthal youngsters had probably long before discovered that a stick with two feathers set at right angles near one end, twirled between the palms and released smartly, would soar upward because of some mysterious lifting power. There is hardly a man living who didn't make his own primitive vertical-flight "machine" before he wore his first necktie.

After da Vinci's day, vertical flight continued to fascinate inventors at least as much as horizontal flight. In 1784 a pair of Frenchmen, a naturalist named Launoy and a mechanic named Bienvenu, not only built a helicopter model but also solved the vexatious problem of torque. They accomplished this with two counter-rotating "rotors," one armed with feathers from the right wings of birds and the other with feathers from left wings. The toy was powered by an ingenious gimmick, a bent bow and wound string, similar to the wound rubber bands of today's model-plane engines.

In mid-19th century, a British nobleman-tinkerer-scientist named Sir George Cayley built a machine based on the Launoy-Bienvenu design, and his notes record that the toy "rose as high as 90 feet in the air." Sir George also built gliders. With the sublime arrogance of the aristocrats of his day, he offered his gardener the honor of making man's first flight in a heavier-than-air machine. The gardener prudently decided that if God had meant for men to fly, He would have made the inventor take the first flight and not a humble man of the soil. Cayley did persuade his coachman to attempt the glider flight, probably in 1852.

Cayley designed and may have actually built a steam-powered helicopter with four 8-bladed rotors to lift and two 4-bladed propellers to pull (a design strikingly similar to the gyroplane), but

In 1862 an unnamed writer published in Paris a prophetic work entitled The Aircraft, a Tool for Lifesaving. *After describing his version of the then-nonexistent helicopter, he went on, ". . . and then I, a modest narrator . . . will have the happiness to see people rescued at sea, and the victims of fires and floods saved by this apparatus."*

the steam engine was too heavy relative to the horsepower delivered to support flight. Engineers today are, nevertheless, impressed by the grasp the English amateur had of vertical-flight principles.

The major obstacle Cayley could not over-

The true pioneer of aerial design was a British aristocrat and amateur of an astonishing range of sciences and political thought named Sir George Cayley. His writings described with startling accuracy the requirements for flight, including as early as 1809 the need for an internal combustion engine that works by "firing the inflammable air generated with a due proportion of common air under a piston." Recently uncovered papers strongly suggest his coachman flew a Cayley-built glider 500 yards in 1852. Cayley's writings described with great accuracy the performance of helicopters once suitable engines became available. This model, built by Paul E. Garber, head curator of the National Air and Space Museum of the Smithsonian Institution, is based on drawings discovered among Cayley's papers.

This craft, built by Louis Bréguet in 1907, lifted two feet off the ground with a very small man at the controls. Was the pilot then the first man to fly a helicopter? Maybe, but four men steadied the apparatus with poles, so some dispute the claim.

come—the lack of a practical engine—stymied flight pioneers until 1903, the year in which Orville and Wilbur Wright built a 4-cylinder gasoline engine and made the first controlled, heavier-than-air flight. The age of aviation was beginning, and the world was ready for vertical flight. But the first successful helicopter flight would require three more decades of experimentation.

Again the French pioneered. Louis Bréguet in 1907 built a cumbersome 4-rotor machine, each rotor armed with four rotating biplane wings. The monstrously complicated device lifted a man two feet but was supported by props and not under control and so was not in true flight. It did little

more than show that new engine technology had made possible manned vertical flight, though that was achievement enough to establish Bréguet as a contributor to the helicopter's invention. He went on to become one of history's greatest designers of fixed-wing craft before returning late in life to experiments with helicopters.

Two months after the Bréguet craft's lift-off, another Frenchman, Paul Cornu, climbed into his 573-pound machine, rose one foot, and moved forward at 6 miles per hour. The craft was unstable, but there is no denying it lifted a pilot and flew forward.

Two months after the "flight" of the Bréguet craft, another Frenchman, Paul Cornu (whose extraordinary name means "horned"—as a beast, with all the implications the conceit carries when applied to men—or else "preposterous"), took off in this machine and rose one foot, to qualify for the world's first uncontested free flight.

Shortly after Cornu's flight, Bréguet produced his second machine. On July 22, 1908, it rose 15 feet and flew some distance under control. Unfortunately, it crashed on landing. Bréguet turned his considerable intellectual powers to fixed-wing craft and became one of the industry's greatest designers.

Enter the giant of vertical flight.

In 1909 a Russian youngster, Igor Sikorsky, on fire with excitement over the infant science of flight, built his first helicopter. Realizing it would not fly, he designed another one the following year. This machine could lift its own weight but was even more unstable than Cornu's machine. Discouraged, Sikorsky turned his genius to conventional aircraft and became one of the true titans of aerial design, working first in his native Russia and later in his adopted United States.

Fortunately, the great Russian did not lose faith in vertical flight. As he explained later:

I did not abandon it. I merely postponed it because I realized that the amount of money and the facilities necessary to solve the helicopter problems were more than I had at my disposal. Another stumbling block was the lack of engines of sufficient power and low weight. I still saw a great potential for the helicopter in the future. I was always against large land areas or runways necessary for the operation of airplanes. To me, a flying machine had to rise and descend vertically, have the ability to stay motionless in the air or fly and maneuver as slow as its pilot desires or the mission calls for.

I could see helicopters carrying people and goods directly to the destination, and not 10 to 15 miles away and then transported there by other means. I also foresaw the helicopter's unparalleled ability as a rescue device under the greatest variety of circumstances. As you know, this has been proven to be true.

Wilbur Wright pronounced the doom of vertical flight: "Like all novices we began with the helicopter (in childhood) but soon saw that it had no future and dropped it. The helicopter does with great labor only what the balloon does without labor, and is no more fitted than the balloon for rapid horizontal flight. If the engine stops, it must fall with deathly violence, for it can neither float like the balloon nor glide like the aeroplane. The helicopter is much easier to design than the aeroplane but it is worthless when done."

It is noteworthy that Sikorsky thought of the helicopter primarily as a lifesaving instrument. Although virtually every one of its designers has stressed the helicopter's value as a rescue craft, paradoxically it is the helicopter's potential as a military vehicle that has paid and probably will always pay for its experimental progress.

In 1916, during World War I, the Central Powers supported the building of a helicopter by Professor Theodore von Kármán and Stefan Petró-czny, a lieutenant in the Austrian Army. With two coaxial and counter-rotating rotors powered by three 120-horsepower engines, the 3,200-pound

Igor Sikorsky in 1909 built the first of a long series of aircraft that were to make him the greatest designer in the history of aeronautics. This 1910 model was not the one that made his reputation, however, for it failed to lift off. Like Bréguet, Sikorsky turned his genius to fixed-wing aircraft, building for his czar the first four-engined airplane (and four-engined bomber) in history, which the 23-year-old designer flew on May 13, 1913.

Emile Berliner, a prolific inventor whose credits include the microphone and a gramaphone, joined with his son Henry, who had learned to fly in the army, to build this "gyrocopter." The machine took off and rose three feet on November 11, 1919, for the first manned flight in the United States. The unwieldy craft had a tendency to rotate because of torque.

craft lifted a pilot, observer, and machine gun more than 150 feet. Von Kármán's machine never slipped the cable that held it to the ground, however, and so was never more than an ingenious kite for carrying an observer.

A U.S. Army-Navy board, reporting to the Secretary of the Navy on December 5, 1917, stated: "The helicopter has been the subject of many experiments in the past, all of which were unsuccessful. Until the efficiency of propellers and the power-weight ratio of engines is radically improved, it is not believed that the helicopter principle is worth developing . . . it is considered that many other more promising developments of direct military bearing should receive prior consideration to helicopters."

In the immediate post-war years, other designers—the Frenchman Douheret and the American father-and-son team of Emile and Henry A. Berliner among them—flew vertical-lift craft with disappointing results.

Despite the continuing setbacks in techno-

After his father retired because of ill health, Henry Berliner removed the wings from a French Nieuport fighter plane, replaced them with struts to hold two rotor blades, and rigged a small rotor near the tail. The rear rotor was to lift the tail so the revolving main rotors would pull at the air at an angle to provide forward as well as vertical motion, an absolute necessity for helicopter design. The craft flew reasonably well at a closed-course demonstration in Washington, D.C., on June 16, 1922, but was unstable. Berliner, like Bréguet and Sikorsky, turned his talents to fixed-wing design.

logical progress, the U.S. Army in 1921 signed a contract with the Russian-born scientist George de Bothezat to build a helicopter at McCook Field, in Dayton, Ohio. Apparently he convinced the army that he had designed a practical helicopter in Russia and could do so again.

Frank Gregory, now a retired brigadier general, was the first American rotary-wing military pilot. In an interview at his home in Tulsa, Oklahoma, General Gregory recounted many delightful anecdotes of those pioneering days, including de Bothezat's unhappy adventures.

A Russian bear in size, de Bothezat had an ego to match. "I am the world's greatest scientist and outstanding mathematician," he once announced. One can only stand in awe of a man

who could make that statement during the era of Einstein, Bertrand Russell, and Alfred North Whitehead, to name only a few of a generation of mathematicians and theoretical physicist-mathematicians whose findings shook the world.

Working in exaggerated secrecy behind canvas walls, de Bothezat was the butt of pranks played by young army pilots working out of McCook Field. They flew low over the fenced-in plot, exciting paranoid fears of spies in the excitable Russian, who roared to the field shaking his fist at the retreating pilots.

On December 18, 1922, he wheeled out a monstrosity with four 6-bladed propellers attached to diagonal crossarms fitted to a pipe framework. There were four smaller propellers: two for hori-

The "flying octopus" design of George de Bothezat, a Russian scientist-mathematician who built the machine for the U.S. Army at McCook Field, in Dayton, Ohio. Beginning in December 1922, the craft took off in a series of flights—on one of these, it lifted the pilot and several other men aboard—but it was uncontrollable and considered too dangerous by the army, which canceled the experiment two years later.

zontal direction control and two, mounted over the engine, to provide a parachute effect to brake descent if the main lift rotors failed.

Piloted by Maj. Thurman H. Bane, the awesome contraption lifted slowly and hovered at six feet for 1 minute, 42 seconds, then drifted helplessly downwind toward a fence. Bane landed the craft on the snow to avoid its becoming entangled in the wire.

De Bothezat's machine made more than 100 test flights over a two-year span. After a larger engine was installed, the craft lifted a pilot and several other persons but it never attained stability.

The army's final report hailed the achievement but was critical of the helicopter's complexity and poor performance. It added ominously, "These features are such as to rule out its development except in the case of such military urgency that the life of the pilot and observer is of little consequence." The report continued with keen insight: "... the future development of the helicopter proper appears to rest rather in the single-screw type, and the reasons for this are at least strong enough to warrant the building and testing of such a type before multiple-screw types are adopted."

Even though the project was abandoned, the army apparently did not rule out further study of vertical flight.

Here and there, other designers were pecking away at the problems of stability and control. In Barcelona, Spain, an aeronautical engineer named Juan de la Cierva struggled with a new concept, a combination of counter-rotating rotors to provide lift and a conventional propeller to provide pull. His first three craft persisted in toppling sideways. Using models powered by rubber bands, he made the momentous discovery that the advancing blade gives more lift than the retreating blade, thus inexorably turning the craft over sideways toward the weaker blade. He solved this problem by hinging the blades and tilting them separately so the advancing blade always had a less advantageous angle than the retreating blade, thereby equalizing lift.

On January 9, 1923, at the Madrid airport, his first model using the new principle flew 600 feet under excellent control. That same month, he flew his C-4 model 2½ miles around a circular course.

Cierva called his invention the Autogiro. It became immensely popular. In 1929 Cierva sold the rights to manufacture the aircraft in the United States to Harold F. Pitcairn of Willow Grove, Pennsylvania.

Although the Cierva machine was a rotary-wing aircraft, it was not a true vertical-lift helicopter. It was a gyroplane, for it depended on the propeller to travel horizontally. The rotors provided lift only when pulled through the air by forward flight. The craft could not lift off vertically, hover, or fly backward or sideward.

Dutch, American, French, Italian, and other Spanish designers built machines that lifted vertically but gave little promise. The true helicopter, depending on engine-driven rotors for both vertical and horizontal motion, still eluded inventors.

Juan de la Cierva, flying his Autogiro on January 9, 1923, near Madrid. The machine's rotors were powered by the passage of air in forward flight, providing only lift but not flight power, and so the craft is not a true helicopter. Nevertheless, it was the first practical rotary-wing craft and went into commercial production in Great Britain and later in the United States.

This helicopter, designed by Corradino d'Ascanio, set an endurance record in 1930 by staying aloft 8 minutes, 45 seconds. It flew 3,538 feet and rose to 59 feet. The rotor blades were hinged so they could find their own most comfortable angle, a principle first used by Cierva on his Autogiro and a significant step forward. The d'Ascanio machine was extraordinarily stable. Unaccountably, d'Ascanio gave up after this promising start.

In September 1931, an Autogiro landed on the U.S.S. *Langley,* the first carrier landing by a
rotary-wing craft.

After a distinguished career designing fixed-wing craft, the Frenchman Bréguet returned to rotary wings and in partnership with René Dorand built this helicopter—they called it the Gyroplane Laboratoire—which took off on June 26, 1935. On December 22, 1935, the craft set an officially recognized speed record of 67 miles per hour. Six months later, a German helicopter took off and was loudly proclaimed as the first successful helicopter—and it still is. Undaunted by his lack of press attention, Bréguet went on setting altitude, duration, and distance records in this machine till World War II.

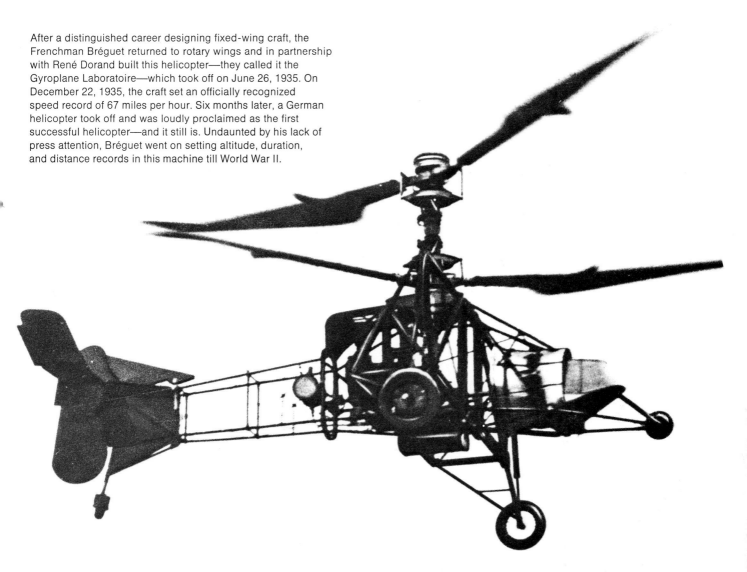

As a working rotary-wing craft, the Autogiro had the field to itself during the late 1920s and early 1930s. In 1931 the U.S. Navy bought three of them; one piloted by Lt. A. M. Pride flew to the aircraft carrier U.S.S. *Langley* on September 23, 1931. The army had three rotary-wing pilots: Lt. Graves H. (Bud) Snyder, 1st Lt. Frank Gregory, and 1st Lt. Erickson S. Nichols.

Accidents plagued the fledgling craft. Flying a field artillery observer at Fort Benning, Georgia, Lieutenant Nichols lost a rotor. Although close to unconsciousness, he bailed out. On ditching the craft, his observer hit the stabilizer and broke an arm.

Amelia Earhart had her troubles with the Autogiro. Trying to take off without enough runway, she would have rammed into a crowd had she not deliberately crashed the machine into a jammed parking lot. Another gyroplane pilot, William Carroll Smith, Jr., tried to develop a technique of landing by stopping in midair and

letting the rotating blades settle him to earth. His technique must have lacked a certain finesse, for he twice crashed on landing. (Ironically, on his way east for more flying lessons, he fell from a hotel window and died.)

Cierva steadily improved the Autogiro, and it sold by the hundreds, but its heyday was over once the helicopter was perfected. Although the gyroplane could not compete as a commercial machine, Cierva's work did advance helicopter theory considerably.

Now there reappears on the scene the brilliant aeronautical designer Bréguet, who built the first machine to "lift" a man back in 1907. After more than two decades of great success with fixed-wing planes, in collaboration with René Dorand he built and flew a twin-rotor helicopter. On December 22, 1935, the French machine set an official speed record of 67 miles per hour. On November 24, 1936, it set an endurance record of 1 hour, 2 minutes and a closed-circuit flight of 27.4 miles.

Nevertheless, when the German-designed Focke-Achgelis Fa-61 took off for a 28-second flight on June 26, 1936—one year after the first French flight—the press, especially in Germany, made a great fanfare about the "first successful controlled helicopter flight." The Fa-61 was a good machine, but when firsts are being handed out, it is hard to ignore the three impressive records of the Bréguet-Dorand helicopter, which clearly antedated the German aircraft's performances.

To cinch the matter of recognition for the Fa-61, its first public demonstration of forward, backward, and sideward flying was performed inside, at the Berlin Sportspalast in February 1938—and the pilot was charming, 90-pound, 5-foot Hanna Reitsch. That did it for the press—the Germans were clearly first.

The true giant of vertical flight meanwhile had already become famous—and wealthy—for his contributions to the development of fixed-wing aircraft. Igor Sikorsky's most notable achievement had been the first multi-engined airplane, which he built and piloted in 1913. Fleeing his homeland in 1918, following the Russian Revolution, he designed aircraft for the French for a brief time.

In 1919 Sikorsky emigrated to the United States. He arrived with only $600 and, through Gen. Billy Mitchell, got a job at McCook Field. When the job ended after six weeks, a kindly commanding officer of the nation's only experi-

One of the main reasons the German Focke-Achgelis Fa-61 got all the press notices as the first successful helicopter is the diminutive and charming Hanna Reitsch, the woman test pilot who in February 1938 publicly demonstrated the craft's controllability by hovering and flying forward, backward, and sideward inside Berlin's Sportspalast.

mental station for aircraft suggested he find other work because aviation was a "dying industry."

Sikorsky supported himself lecturing while he scratched together money to start his own aviation company.

With small contributions from his students and those who attended his lectures, on March 5, 1923, he founded the Sikorsky Aero Engineering Corporation. Lacking sufficient funds, the company struggled to perfect a twin-engined transport plane, the S-29-A (the "A" for "America"). The workers rummaged through junkyards and five-and-ten-cent stores to secure parts and materials. Even a windfall of $5,000 from the great Russian composer Sergei Rachmaninoff, who accepted the vice-presidency of the corporation, barely carried the S-29-A through to completion.

Igor Sikorsky returned to rotary-wing craft after a brilliant career designing long-range airplanes, especially amphibians for ocean travel. Conscious that control problems had bothered all previous designers, he practiced on a test rig.

Several airplane designs followed, which bettered the company's finances. Finally, in 1928, Sikorsky built the amphibian plane S-38. The best amphibian of its day, it was an immediate success.

So well received was the S-38 that Pan American Airways contracted for a 40-passenger flying boat, the S-40. Sikorsky made the S-40's maiden voyage from Miami to the Panama Canal, with waystops at Cuba, Jamaica, and Colombia. The pilot, incidentally, was Charles A. Lindbergh, a close friend and adviser of Sikorsky's. The flight led to new contracts and, finally, to a flying boat, the S-42, that crossed the Atlantic in 1937.

Though he had devoted almost three decades to fixed-wing aircraft, Sikorsky had never lost interest in helicopters. He was just "too busy otherwise to do anything about them." He tells why and how he got back into his original field, vertical flight.

As aviation progressed, airplanes became better in nearly every respect. With respect to takeoff, however, airplanes were steadily becoming worse and worse and worse. Knowing that the airplane is completely hopeless with respect to short landings, I continued to think about the helicopter. However, having learned enough about flying, I realized that the helicopter represented such a difficult problem that one should either give the whole, so to say, intellect and soul to fight it through to success or not start at all.

Sikorsky knew that most engineers thought a truly controllable helicopter was impossible. Some of them said that even if it were possible, the helicopter would have no use.

On January 14, 1938, a navy document stated: "Rotoplanes might be of some use in antisubmarine work when operated from auxiliaries. This appears to be a minor application which hardly justifies expenditure of experimental funds at present." Captain Walter S. Diehl, the navy's chief aerodynamicist, went on record with a prediction that no helicopter would ever carry a useful load.

Sikorsky disagreed: "I said that the helicopter will do a number of jobs which no airplane will do. I thought about it all the time . . . from 1938 I

decided to make every effort to return and this time to build a successful helicopter."

And then Sikorsky explained his almost mystic compulsion to return to the vertical-lift concept, despite his overwhelming success as a builder of conventional aircraft.

I had every conviction that the helicopter would prove a unique and extremely effective . . . instrumentality for saving lives. It had to me a sort of romantic or philosophical appeal. The appeal is this: what kind of a gadget . . . can give you unlimited freedom of transportation? If a man is in need, well, the airplane can come in and throw some flowers on him and that's just about all. A direct lift aircraft could come in and save his life. Direct lift aircraft can go anywhere anytime where there is air—and this commodity is fairly widespread over our wonderful globe. Even if the helicopter cannot land . . . the helicopter can use a hoist . . . or a cable and can contact anyplace on the ground, on a roof, on water, on a treetop, absolutely anyplace.

The Sikorsky company had become a subsidiary of United Aircraft Corporation in 1929. In February 1939, the parent company gave Sikorsky the go-ahead to design a helicopter. Within an astonishingly short time—only six months—he had a model ready for trial.

"I was not only the designer but the test pilot of this aircraft during the first flight," Sikorsky recalled.

On the momentous date of September 14, 1939, Sikorsky and his helicopter lifted off and hovered, though the craft was tethered to prevent it rising too high. Sikorsky reported his reactions.

The fundamental goal of an airplane pilot is to attain rapid enough ground motion to be airborne. Speed and flight, to the airplane pilot, are completely

On September 14, 1939, Sikorsky made his first flight in the VS-300. Although the craft was tethered to weights under the landing gear struts to keep it from rising to dangerous heights before control problems were solved, this first flight excited the inventor enormously and spurred him on.

inseparable. But no such primary "sense" of coalition is true of the helicopter pilot. On my first helicopter flights, I got into the air just a few inches, then a few feet. The ground did not race past me. Landmarks held their distance. The VS-300 was motionless, although it was airborne, except for unexpected and minor shifting of the craft in some direction—often a direction that occasioned my total surprise.

I was aloft but I wasn't going any place. If you have had 30 years of fixed-wing flying behind you, the sensation in your first helicopter flight, then, is pretty novel. My years of experience kept saying to me, "Why aren't we moving? We are airborne, certainly." Then the engineer seemed to reply, "Don't be absurd. You are doing precisely what you set out to do. Remember, hovering is one of the characteristics you sought in this aircraft." Presently the craft would veer slightly. It was not easy to determine whether this was caused by a too difficult control arrangement or by total lack of experience piloting a helicopter.

Difficulty with the controls forced 18 changes of configuration in the aircraft. In December 1939, a gust of wind toppled the machine and smashed the rotor. The pilot, Serge Gluhareff, escaped injury. Sikorsky went back to the old drawing board.

"By spring of 1940," he said, "I could stay in the air as long as 15 minutes, coming down when I wanted to. Better and longer flights were made with very satisfactory control in hovering, rearward and sidewise flight. The controls were poor, however, in forward flight."

Sikorsky faced the embarrassing difficulty with sublime calm. When a vice-president of United Aircraft asked why he saw many movies of flights moving in every direction but forward, Sikorsky replied, "Forward flight is a minor engineering problem we haven't solved as yet." As Sikorsky had predicted, by spring of 1941 the experimental

VS-300 was flying forward at 70 miles per hour.

In 1941 Sikorsky built a single helicopter for the army, a much modified version of the VS-300. Designated the XR-4, it was twice as large and powerful as its prototype. Tests with the VS-300 continued meanwhile, and as each bug in the craft was corrected, the change was incorporated in the XR-4.

The XR-4 was first test-flown in January 1942, and in April Sikorsky showed off his tricks at Stratford, Connecticut, for a governmental interagency board. Among the board's members was Wing Commander Reggie Brie of the British Royal Air Force, a rotary-wing pilot who had flown gyroplanes off the Italian cruiser *Fiume* in 1935. He was interested in having the helicopter ride merchant ships in the deadly struggle against German U-boats that were threatening to strangle embattled Britain.

Sikorsky's test pilot, Les Morris, took off vertically, zigzagged through rows of trees, sped off toward the horizon and returned, cut off power to glide on autorotating blades, and recovered power. He hovered and let down a rope ladder. An assistant climbed the ladder and pulled it up after him. The pilot climbed into the clouds. Out of sight of the observers—fortunately—he suffered an engine failure and began to fall. The autorotating blades came to his rescue, however, and he made a power-off landing that looked like part of the show.

The observers, especially the British pilot, were impressed by the craft's performance. The big brass, however, remained sluggish about pushing the strange machine. It would take much more than a single demonstration to convince them of the helicopter's potential as a military vehicle.

On May 13, 1942, Les Morris climbed into the XR-4 and prepared to take off on the first cross-country delivery flight of a helicopter. The army was to take delivery of the XR-4 at Wright Field (formerly McCook Field), in Dayton. Virtually every move he made in the next few days

Still tethered, and with Sikorsky at the controls, the modified VS-300 (top left) performed well and encouraged him to attack the endurance record, which he broke in May 1941. The VS-300A (bottom). In an abortive experiment, Sikorsky tried tandem rotors but abandoned the principle, returning to the single rotor. The pilot is Les Morris, who later made the first cross-country delivery of a military helicopter.

The final form of the VS-300 that persuaded the army to order a larger version, designated the XR-4—the first helicopter in the U.S. armed services.

would set a new record of some kind, for everything he did would be a first in aviation history.

Morris wrote the story of his epoch-making flight.

"Mr. Sikorsky hovered near, nervously chewing at the corner of his mouth. His keen gray-blue eyes flashed out from under the familiar gray fedora as they searched every detail of the craft to detect any sign of flaw that might develop. I knew the capacity of those eyes from experience—the time they had seen from 50 feet a strut that was so slightly bent that I had to sight along it at close range to notice it; the time when, without apparently looking at the ship at all, he had commented on a tail-rotor blade whose tip had an eighth-of-an-inch nick in it.

"And I knew on this May morning that his vision would be doubly sharp because he was not wholly convinced of the wisdom of this flight—he felt that this 'first-of-the-type' should be handled with kid gloves and should be delivered to Dayton by highway truck."

Sikorsky could find no flaw and reluctantly gave Morris the signal to take off.

"The engine labored and roared its crescendo as I pulled upward on the pitch control to rise off the ground. The ship lifted vertically to 10 or 15 feet, then I eased forward on the stick and we started off across the field. Sweeping in a gentle circle, we swooped low over the clump of up-turned faces and waving hands, then on over the factory in an easy climb to 1,500 feet. A car with a large yellow dot painted on the roof was already speeding out the factory gate—it was to be my shadow for five days.

"I quickly lost them in the elm-tunnels of Stratford, but my maps were marked with the exact route they would take, so I followed it closely, always ready to land in some little field beside the road should the slightest thing seem wrong. They would then see me as they drove by, and delays would be minimized."

Morris and the chase car had agreed on a route and a speed of 60 miles per hour for the helicopter. When a headwind blew, the car often outstripped the aircraft.

Morris began ticking off firsts. Near Brewster, New York, he flew across a state border for the first time. The wooded area worried him, and he edged southward.

"From the 2,500 feet of altitude where I now flew, there was an unbroken stretch of forest. The highway to the south at least offered promise of speedy assistance in case of trouble, so its winding ribbon became my temporary beacon."

In the early days of America's part in World War II, civilians had set up a network of sky watchers with the naive hope of spotting enemy aircraft before they could work any mischief. Les amused himself by imagining the kind of reports they were telephoning headquarters as his weird craft passed overhead. One caller reported that a windmill had just flown by.

Despite the gravity of the mission, the prankish Morris delighted in horrifying crowds unused to the tricks a helicopter could perform. At the Albany, New York, airport, he ignored the landing strip and flew over a line of parked planes, heading for a collision with a fence. Feet short of a collision, he stopped dead in the air, pivoted languidly on the axis of the rotor strut, and settled to land with his nose almost against the hangar door. The shaken spectators recovered slowly.

On the next leg, he flew over the pastoral Mohawk Valley at only 200 feet.

"Dooryards full of chickens and farm animals would suddenly become uninhabited as shelter was sought from this strange hawk—but the yards would quickly fill again as houses and barns ejected motley groups of human beings gaping skywards."

This pioneer flight, incidentally, was supposedly being conducted in top secrecy, that beloved secrecy military bureaucrats fondly believe in. The farmers of the Mohawk Valley could hardly be expected to keep locked within their bosoms the news of the strange vessel that had clattered through their skies.

Morris ended the first day at Syracuse. The day had gone well, except for a vexing problem with the transmission gear train.

While test-flying the first army XR-4, Les Morris noticed that his engineer passenger was busy with notes on a clipboard. He took off vertically and mischievously soared straight up one mile without forward movement. When the engineer looked out to see what progress they had made, he was astonished to see they had been flying for minutes and were still over the takeoff spot. "It's a lie!" he shouted.

"It seemed strange that we should create a totally novel aircraft and run into no particular structural, functional, or control problems—whereas a simple gear transmission, something that had been developed and used successfully in hundreds of millions of applications during the last half century, was destined to hound our every move."

The next day Morris approached the control tower at the Rochester airport.

"No ship may land without first receiving a green light signal from the control tower operator. It was fortunate indeed for me that my ship could hang motionless in the air, because when I whirred up in front of the tower and looked the man in the face, he was so astounded that he completely neglected his duty and left me hovering there for the better part of a minute before he stopped rubbing his eyes and, with a broad grin, flashed on the green light. Quickly and gently, then, I settled to a landing at the base of the tower."

On the flight to Buffalo, Morris lost the chase car. He was worried about an approaching storm and looked not for a landing field, as he would have in a conventional plane, but for a house with a fairly large lawn and wires indicating a telephone.

"I failed to pick up the yellow dot on the highway for reasons I cannot understand (they claimed I flew directly over them several times), and after five or 10 minutes the storm was close enough so I didn't want it any closer. I swung in,

Right, top: A heavy load readied for a lift to an offshore drilling rig. Helicopters servicing the oil rigs cut work hours and expenses so drastically they pay for themselves in a short time. Right, bottom: Spraying a forest in the Pacific Northwest to kill a runaway infestation of hemlock loopers.

This historic photograph shows the XR-4 on its delivery to the army in Dayton, Ohio, after Les Morris flew it from Connecticut. Sikorsky is shaking hands with Col. Frank Gregory, the first American military pilot to fly a helicopter and a lifelong enthusiast for rotary-wing craft. The smiling gentleman in the center is Orville Wright, who with his brother Wilbur first considered inventing the helicopter before discarding it in favor of inventing the airplane.

then, slowly over a nice green strip of grass about 75 feet wide between two ploughed gardens. On one side of the gardens was a comfortable old farmhouse.

"The folks in the old farmhouse were only too glad to let me use their phone. The owner—in his late 70s and on crutches—had been out in the chicken house when I settled in for the landing and was full of suggestions as to what had gone wrong with the engine, because he had heard it 'sputter and backfire' when I came over. I don't believe he ever became quite convinced that the landing was intentional."

The ground party arrived by car while Morris was on the phone.

"When it cleared and we were preparing to leave again, one of the men warned me quite persistently of a hidden ditch about 200 feet from the ship. I couldn't make him believe that I would take off straight up."

At the Buffalo airport, Les Morris deliberately overshot the runway by 20 feet and backed onto it to astonish the crowd and further lessen the possibility of keeping the flight and the craft's capabilities secret.

After a stop at Erie, Pennsylvania, it was on to Cleveland, Ohio. The control tower operator at the Cleveland airport flashed the green light at Morris, who ignored the landing strip as usual and floated along the front of the hangar looking for an empty slot.

"As I meandered along 50 feet in the air, the green light still followed me. He held the light until I got close to the tower and then finally gave up. I hovered momentarily out in front of him grinning to see what he would do. He was scratching his head—reached for the light again, thought better of it, and finally with both hands signaled me vigorously down."

Sikorsky met Morris in Cleveland and continued with him to Mansfield, Ohio, serving as copilot. Several others of the chase-car crew had been passengers during earlier laps.

When the XR-4 touched down at Wright Field on May 18, it had flown 761 air-miles in 16 hours, 10 minutes, and had made 16 landings. Among those welcoming the XR-4 at Wright Field was Orville Wright, who with his brother Wilbur had first considered inventing the helicopter but abandoned it as hopeless in favor of inventing the fixed-wing airplane.

2

First Tottering Steps

Successfully completing rigid and exhaustive test flights, the Sikorsky XR-4 was redesignated the YR-4. It became the first production helicopter when the Army Air Corps ordered 29 and Britain's Royal Air Force 15. The army lent one to the still unenthusiastic U.S. Navy. With full production, the "Y" was dropped, the R-4 becoming the first in a series of constantly improved vehicles. Encouraged by Sikorsky's success, other helicopter designers pressed forward with their experiments.

Among the brass who had witnessed a demonstration of precision flying of the Sikorsky XR-4 in June 1942—with the Old Man himself as the pilot—was Comdr. Frank A. Erickson of the U.S. Coast Guard. He was deeply excited by the craft's potential and for the same idealistic reason as Sikorsky—it was the possibilities for rescue that seized his imagination. Other officers recommended use of the new machine. Early in 1943, Adm. Ernest J. King, commander in chief of the U.S. Fleet and chief of Naval Operations, made development of the helicopter's seagoing capabilities a responsibility of the Coast Guard. Virtually all the choppers the navy purchased during World War II were used by the Coast Guard. Commander Erickson became the service's first helicopter pilot.

Nevertheless, it was an army pilot, the helicopter enthusiast Col. Frank Gregory, who, on May 6, 1943, made the first helicopter landing on the deck of a ship—the U.S.S. *Bunker Hill.* The next morning, for the edification of 97 high-ranking officers and key civilians, he took off again and in a stiff wind landed on the deck while the ship was under way. The U.S. Navy was still not sold on the helicopter's military value. But Britain's RAF was; it pushed a vigorous program of anti-submarine warfare experiments with helicopters riding merchant vessels.

Early in 1944, the U.S. Navy had reason to be grateful to those who had persisted in developing rotary-wing craft. On January 3 of that year, the destroyer U.S.S. *Turner,* anchored off Sandy Hook, New Jersey, burst into flames following an explosion felt 15 miles away. A second explosion 47 minutes later sank the vessel. The survivors, many hideously burned, were dying at the Sandy Hook hospital for lack of blood plasma. With a 25-knot northeaster blowing snow and sleet, fixed-wing pilots at Floyd Bennett Field in New York City did not dare to take off on the mercy mission.

But Commander Erickson chanced it, and lifting his R-4 into the storm, he raced to the Battery at the southern tip of Manhattan to pick up the plasma. To take on the overweight load (some 100 burned sailors awaited the lifesaving plasma), Erickson had to ditch his copilot, Lt. (jg.) Walter Bolton. Reporting on the mission, the *New York Times* editorialized: ". . . nothing can dim the future of a machine which can take in its

Sikorsky did not have the field to himself. Frank N. Piasecki followed close behind with his designs, including this PV-2, which he is piloting. He made his first flight in the craft on April 11, 1943.

A truly important newcomer to the helicopter community was the Bell Aircraft Company (now Bell Helicopter Company), which switched from fighter planes to rotary-wing construction. Here a Bell Model 30 is experimenting with crop dusting.

This Coast Guard helicopter is landing on a ship at sea to test the craft's rescue possibilities. The first landing on a seagoing vessel had been made the year before, in 1943.

stride weather conditions such as those which prevailed in New York on Monday."

It is especially appropriate that this first helicopter rescue mission in history was flown by Commander Erickson in a craft designed by Igor Sikorsky, both of whom were among the foremost supporters of vertical flight for its rescue potential.

With a savage war being fought on all the world's seas, the U.S. Navy was more interested in the helicopter's use as a weapon—an antisubmarine vehicle—than as a lifesaver. On January 6, 1944, the British merchant ship M.V. *Dagestan,* sailing from New York Harbor in a convoy, carried an R-4 to try helicopter lift-offs and landings on the high seas. Those in charge could not have posed a sterner test. Not only was the *Dagestan* a natural dog as a seagoing vessel, with a built-in roll of at least 10 degrees in the calmest seas, but its grain cargo had shifted, giving the vessel a permanent five-degree list. (One unsupported source says a convoy patrolled by three R-4s sailed from New York on January 2, 1944.)

Lieutenant (jg.) Stewart Graham of the Coast Guard braved the 20-knot wind and dangerous roll to make the first flight from a ship in mid-Atlantic. Conditions the next day were worse, but Flight Lt. "Jeep" Cable of the RAF was so seasick that he volunteered to fly just to get off the plunging ship and settle his stomach during a "restful" test flight.

The pilots reported that the R-4 had insufficient power to operate safely from a rolling vessel. Skeptics immediately recommended junking the antisubmarine program; enthusiasts recommended building a more powerful helicopter.

As the end of World War II approached, it became obvious that the helicopter would not be ready for effective antisubmarine work. But the vertical-lift craft's potential for other uses brought in a flood of calls to the Coast Guard.

On September 14, 1944, a vicious hurricane (unnamed because it was before the era of girlish monickers for killer winds) smashed the East Coast from North Carolina through New England, registering 134 miles per hour at Cape Henry, Virginia. Because shipping lanes were jammed with wartime convoys, the death toll at sea reached 344. Land communications broke down throughout Long Island.

The commander of the Long Island Coast Guard station was Capt. Eugene Osborne, a noted lifesaving expert. Even the governmentese of his report cannot disguise his enthusiasm for the rescue work performed by his four helicopters during the hurricane and for the chopper's lifesaving role in general.

"It is believed," he wrote, "that helicopters stationed at strategically located points along the coast, such as important lifeboat stations, would prove to be of inestimable value in connection with Coast Guard work. . . . This is particularly true in view of the development of the other lifesaving phases of the helicopter such as the lifting of personnel from the water or ground to the plane through the use of an electric winch, which, when perfected, should prove a most useful supplement to the other Coast Guard facilities."

By the end of that year, all military services were fitting their helicopters with electric hoists for lifesaving purposes.

Several military units claim the honor of the first behind-the-lines rescue by helicopter. Probably the First Air Commando Group, based in India and commanded by the famed Col. Philip D. Cochran, has the best claim. The air commandos, stationed in enemy territory, operated in support of Gen. Orde C. Wingate's Raiders in the Burmese jungles.

In April 1944, according to the army report—which referred to the rescue mission as the "first use of the helicopter . . . behind enemy lines"—a light plane with four men aboard crashed behind the Japanese lines in Burma. Besides the pilot, the plane carried two wounded soldiers and one with malaria. All four survived the crash, but they had come down in an area inaccessible to rescue planes. Messages dropped to the stranded men instructed them to climb up a ridge to await help.

Lieutenant (jg.) Barney Mazonson took off in an R-4 to act as a target for radar calibration of the U.S.S. Bennington, *the newly commissioned carrier anchored in Gravesend Bay, off New York City. He had no radio, so he landed on the ship's flight deck to get his instructions. As he put it when he reported to his superiors on his reception: "All hell broke loose when the helicopter touched down."*

Now, the landing of the first aircraft on a new carrier is a very big deal indeed and calls for much ceremony. The captain came roaring onto the flight deck in a rage because the ugly little stepchild of the skies had claimed the great honor and spoiled the gaudy dedication show that was scheduled. He ordered the helicopter to leave—that is, as soon as his ship had been rigged for flight operations by having its antennas lowered, and so forth. Lieutenant Mazonson did not hang about during the embarrassing preparations for evicting him and his unappreciated aircraft; he lifted from the deck and took off backward, dipping out of sight over the side as soon as he could and slinking along at wavetop level back to his base.

Colonel Cochran ordered an R-4 flown in from India. When the helicopter arrived, the men were told to move down to a small rice paddy. The R-4, piloted by 1st Lt. Carter Harman, lifted them out one by one.

Although the R-4 was designed for one passenger, on later evacuation missions Harman often carried out two at a time. The rescues were made under harrowing circumstances. Besides the ever-present enemy fire, he had mechanical problems with the helicopter, which was one of the first production models. Harman's rescue flights earned him the Distinguished Flying Cross.

Colonel Cochran had been instrumental in his unit's being assigned four R-4s when they were still hard to come by. But only one was service-

Sergeant L. F. Goins models a German kite-helicopter that was trailed behind U-boats on a 1,000-foot cable and telephone line. Should the submarine be forced to crash dive, the observer could jettison the rotors and unfurl the parachute strapped to the post behind his back. What he did for an encore alone on the surface of the cruel sea is not clear.

able—the others were damaged en route or had parts missing.

"Just imagine what we could do with a couple hundred of them," Cochran said after witnessing the rescue missions.

Tokyo Rose described the machine as "a new form of Yankee frightfulness." Nevertheless, when 15 Zeroes raided the air base in Burma where Lieutenant Harman's lone helicopter sat exposed on the tarmac, they shot up every plane on the field and destroyed every bottle of rum in the commissary—but they ignored the strange looking rotary-wing craft, probably because it looked like a plane that had already crashed and lost its wings.

To test a sonar-equipped helicopter, a pilot took off from the U.S.S. Cobb *near Block Island, Rhode Island, and tried to hover. He found he needed a point of reference on the water to keep him from drifting. His rotor wash blew away float lights and dyes. On a hunch, he dropped the comic section of the Sunday paper into the water. It turned instantly soggy so it didn't drift; the bright colors made it easy to hold in view. The helicopter detected and tracked the target submarine. Experts judged the sonar head good enough for further development, thanks to the Katzenjammer Kids.*

Tour operators around the world have discovered the splendid sight-seeing opportunities offered by the helicopter. A Bell 47 of the Kauai Helicopters Company carries honeymooning couples to remote and otherwise inaccessible beaches on the Hawaiian island of Kauai. The Bell 47 was the first chopper to win certification for commercial service.

In late April 1945, a Royal Canadian Air Force PBY-5A crashed 180 miles south of Goose Bay, Labrador. Two of the men aboard suffered burns. After a search of several days, a U.S. Air Transport C-54 spotted the wreckage. Two RCAF planes equipped with skis landed on the snow and took out the injured men. A blizzard halted further rescue. When the planes tried to land again after the storm, the snow was too soft and deep. The nine survivors settled down to wait—perhaps weeks—till nearby lakes had thawed enough for floatplanes to land.

The U.S. Coast Guard at New York City knocked down an R-4, loaded it into a C-54, and sent it to Goose Bay. Lieutenant August Kleisch flew the reassembled helicopter to a camp close to the crash site. He found the airmen in a cozy tunnel they had burrowed 10 feet into the snow. Kleisch brought them out in nine trips.

On November 29, 1945, a barge ran onto Penfield Reef near Bridgeport, Connecticut. Seas ran too high for a rescue by boat. Summoned by police, Sikorsky's chief test pilot and nephew of Igor's, D. D. (Jimmy) Viner, took off in one of the new R-5s, which were equipped with rescue hoists. In heavy rain and winds gusting to 60 miles per hour, Viner and his hoist operator, Capt. Jackson Beighle of the Army Air Force, brought the men ashore.

Although the end of the war was disastrous for the helicopter industry, several designers produced important new craft. Charles H. Kaman resigned from the helicopter division of United Aircraft to work on a revolutionary design using two counter-rotating and intermeshing rotors mounted on separate twin booms. He was quoted as saying that once production was adequate, he could sell his helicopters for the price of a medium-sized automobile. In short, he was talking about a Model T of vertical-lift craft, a dream that has haunted the industry from the beginning and is no nearer realization than it was in the 1940s.

The Bell Aircraft Company on March 8, 1946, won CAA (Civil Aeronautics Administra-

Colonel H. R. Sullivan and Capt. Ed Stevenson of the Army Air Force, flying an R-5 in Alaska, came across a moose fighting off a wolf pack. They hovered only a few feet over the moose, but the wolves were not impressed. Colonel Sullivan got their attention by shooting the pack leader with a carbine. The other wolves took the hint. Captain Stevenson landed and skinned the wolf before leaving.

tion) certification for the first commercial helicopter in history, the superb Model 47. The Bell 47 promptly began gathering world records and turned up in more than 40 countries, doing yeoman service for police and rescue units.

In the predawn hours of September 20, 1946, a Sabena airlines DC-4 with 37 passengers and a crew of seven aboard, most of them Belgians, approached Gander, Newfoundland, after a transatlantic crossing. The ceiling was down to 400 feet, but the pilot had little choice about landing. The plane dipped too low, and 25 miles short of the runway, it crashed through the spruce forest to the soggy muskeg floor below.

The stewardess shrieked in French, "Get out of here! Quick!" Of the 18 survivors only five could move, and they pulled the others from the plane. Flames licked at the wing tanks. "Farther into the woods," the stewardess screamed. "Farther!"

Floundering in the oozing muskeg, the ablebodied dragged their injured companions into the woods, far enough to be clear of the explosion that followed.

One of the survivors, Helen Ruth Henderson, gave the following account of their plight.

"Those who could walk looked after the others. They were able to find some extra things to put over us. Some said they were going to see if they could find help. They scouted around . . . and came back.

"By the first afternoon, we were all together . . . 18 [of us]. Someone built a fire, and we sat around it in a semicircle. We talked to give courage to one another. And we sang. I sang the doxology. No one else seemed to know it. So I sang it alone.

"We tried to keep the fire going for a signal. The plane was still burning and sending up sparks. We thought someone might see . . . but [by] the afternoon of the second day, we were beginning to get discouraged.

"It was so strange . . . the realization that with all the modern-day communication facilities, we were here in the woods and couldn't communicate with people. We were lost."

When the airliner's radio had gone off the air, the U.S. Coast Guard Air-Sea Rescue Base at Argentia, on the southern coast of Newfoundland, was alerted. Several PBY amphibian planes began the search for the missing airliner.

Miss Henderson's story continues.

"We could hear planes coming and going, and every time we heard one we would strain for it to come closer. But it would leave us. Then . . . there was one we could tell was nearer us. It seemed lower, and the engine was stronger. As soon as it circled, we knew we had been found.

"Another plane returned in a few minutes and dropped us food and water and medicine. The stewardess made us all swallow a large pill. We ate our food slowly and very sparingly. We didn't have a great deal because supplies had only been dropped for five of us. I guess the pilots couldn't see the rest of us for the trees."

Then an incredible thing happened. Two trappers stumbled across the wreckage and the survivors. They built a fire and made some tea for the group. Then they sauntered off about their business, never to be heard from again, leaving 13 desperately injured people to their private agony.

But the survivors were not alone much longer. A rescue party of 14 men from the Air Transport Command, led by army doctor Capt. Samuel P. Martin and a Newfoundland guide, were flown in PBY amphibians to a rocky stream that flowed to within a mile of the crash site. They inflated rubber rafts and floated five and a half hours through rapids to where the overhead plane signaled them to go ashore and strike inland. It took another hour to walk the last mile.

"We heard a yell and saw flashlights in the woods. And here came the men from Fort McAndrew!" Miss Henderson said.

"Captain Martin was able to give morphine to those who were suffering. Unless you have been lying on cold sod and roots for hours and hours, you have no idea what the soldiers meant to us, not only for our courage and morale, but in relief from physical pain."

The torque of the main rotor tends to make a helicopter revolve around its axis. To combat torque in pioneering days, designers resorted to many strange devices. This rotary-wing craft, built by United Helicopters, Incorporated, in 1947, blew a jet thrust through vanes at the end of the stovepipe fuselage to counteract the twist of the rotor.

Captain Martin faced a grim problem. Having made the bone-grinding trip in, he realized that most of the injured would not survive the same kind of trip out. Government and military authorities decided that only helicopters could do the job.

Back in the States, Capt. Richard Burke, the Coast Guard's eastern area rescue officer, asked for two Air Force C-54 transports. He ordered the disassembly of a Coast Guard R-6 at Elizabeth City, North Carolina, and of an army R-4 in New York City. The next morning, both helicopters arrived in Gander aboard the C-54s. Early in the afternoon, Lieutenant Kleisch, the pilot who had rescued the RCAF crash survivors in the same general area 16 months earlier, took off and sped toward the crash scene at 90 miles per hour.

Captain Martin and his men had gone 48 hours without sleep and looked forward with dread to carrying the injured survivors on litters a quarter-mile to the helicopter clearing. They were not sure their exhausted bodies would stand up to the brutal job of slogging through the knee-deep ooze.

Suddenly, like the U.S. Cavalry at the Saturday matinee, a party of hardy Newfoundlanders led by woods veteran Jim Johns burst upon the scene. They had already walked six miles through the muskeg, but the tough islanders carried the victims to the plateau where the R-6 hovered above the soggy ground.

When Kleisch tried to land, his craft sank into the ooze up to its belly. To provide a platform, a PBY amphibian at Gander took on a load of lumber and pushed it out over the clearing. The ground force threw together a rude platform strong enough to support the helicopter.

Lieutenant Kleisch began ferrying the injured to a lake where three PBYs transferred them to the Gander hospital only 20 minutes away. Before dark Kleisch had brought out eight of the most seriously hurt survivors. The other helicopter had been damaged in unloading, repaired in time for late afternoon duty, then damaged again when a spectator ran dangerously close to the whirling rotors, causing the pilot to slam on the rotor brake. The too-violent braking sheared the drive system safety pins. Because of the onlooker's goof, the other litter cases had to spend an extra night in the swamp.

The next day, the helicopters brought out the remaining survivors, the rescue team, the Newfoundlanders, and Gilbert Perier, president of Sabena, who had flown in to help with the rescue.

Kaman developed a helicopter especially designed for fire fighting. Pilots quickly learned they could blow away flames with their downwash, permitting firemen to approach the base of the fire with suppressants.

Modern-day ice pilots find it hard to believe that explorers once braved Arctic and Antarctic seas without helicopter help. Operation High Jump used helicopters for ice navigation in the Antarctic in 1946–47. Here a chopper sets down on the U.S.S. *Glacier* during Operation Deep Freeze.

The dead were buried on the spot. Funeral services were read in a transport plane flying over the site.

At the other end of the world, in Antarctica, a naval task force was working its way through the ice toward the continental shoreline during Operation High Jump, a large-scale American exploration of the globe's southernmost and least hospitable region. Leading the flotilla—one of three groups involved in High Jump—was the U.S. Coast Guard icebreaker *Northwind*. The icebreaker's skipper, Capt. Charles W. Thomas,

Helicopters began fighting forest fires about 1948. Pilots quickly learned that the chopper's downwash can blow smoke and flames away from fire fighters so they can walk up to the edge of the fire with water and foam. On an island near Seattle, Washington, a police helicopter used the downwash to blow the fire into the sea. "I just herded the fire down to the water like sheep," the pilot said.

The Kaman 225 was the world's first turbine-powered helicopter and in this configuration was used for agricultural dusting and spraying. This landmark model is now installed in the Smithsonian Institution.

reported on the value of his helicopter in ice navigation.

"In a well-organized ice convoy, the commander needs to know what his ships will encounter within the next day. The skipper of the icebreaker is interested in the picture within the next hour or two and the officer of the deck, within his own range of visibility. In Operation High Jump, the admiral had no means of making a long-range reconnaissance. Hence, helicopter reconnaissance within a radius of 25 miles was essential.

"The Central Group began working its way through the pack on December 31, 1946. It reached its destination, the Bay of Whales, on January 17, 1947. Battering a track through 650

miles of ice in 18 days would not have been possible without helicopter reconnaissance."

When the submarine *Sennet* ran into trouble, the *Northwind* had to tow it to safety and return to the convoy in the shortest possible time. Without the icebreaker, the other ships were in danger of being crushed by the ice. A helicopter guided the icebreaker out and back to the flotilla just in time to save two cargo ships already badly holed.

Of the four navy helicopters taking part in Operation High Jump, two were lost. One crashed into the sea, giving the pilot and observer a very cold bath indeed. Lieutenant Commander Walter Sessums gives his account as pilot of the second downed aircraft.

"On January 19, 1947, I took off from the

Pine Island with Capt. [George J.] Dufek for an ice recco and photo hop. When we took off, the weather was fine. About 50 miles from the ship, the weather suddenly clobbered up and we headed back, flying through rain, snow, sleet, etc. The 'copter took on such a load of ice that I couldn't even see through the Plexiglas and had to fly with my head out of the door. About a quarter-mile from the ship, it gave up the ghost and quit flying from the load of ice. Dufek and I spent about eight minutes in the water (temp. 28°) without 'poopey suits' until fished out by a crash boat."

The navy pilots showed tremendous stamina, for it is an axiom of cold-water navigation that even young athletes rarely live longer than five minutes in Arctic or Antarctic waters.

Despite his near-fatal dunking, Captain Dufek used many helicopters when as rear admiral he returned to the Antarctic in 1956, first as commander of the U.S. naval force and later of the entire U.S. expedition in Operation Deep Freeze.

The first official demonstration of seagoing helicopters before high-ranking navy brass occurred aboard the U.S.S. *Franklin D. Roosevelt* in 1947. The flier was Sikorsky's chief test pilot, Jimmy Viner. Before the dazzled eyes of observers, he made real-life rescues of four pilots who crashed during the exercises. The first airman he picked up was Lt. Frank A. Shields. At one rescue, Viner had to dip his nose wheel into the sea so that his assistant could pull aboard an unconscious and drowning pilot. Jimmy Viner's demonstration was extremely persuasive to all witnesses—especially the airmen fished out of the cruel sea. Shields, who was the first navy pilot to be saved at sea by helicopter, switched from fixed-wing to rotary-wing craft and qualified as a helicopter pilot in March 1952.

At the explosion of the test atomic bomb at Bikini Atoll in the Pacific, military observers thoughtfully watched the fireball devour the vast flotilla of sacrificial vessels anchored about the lagoon. It did not take a chalk talk to persuade those present that the day of massed amphibious assaults was over. In July 1947, the chief of Naval Operations set down requirements for helicopter transport of assault troops from carriers, the first step in what became the Marine Corps' vertical-assault doctrine.

At the time, however, the largest helicopter was the Sikorsky HO3S-1, capable of carrying a pilot and two Marines with battle equipment, hardly an overwhelming strike force. But bigger and vastly improved choppers were on the way.

By 1949 a new generation of helicopters had appeared, and besides the Bell 47 four other craft had been approved by the CAA for civilian use: the Sikorsky 51 and Sikorsky 52, the Hiller 360, and the Kaman 190.

All those craft were superb instruments, far ahead of the pioneer helicopters that had already made themselves indispensable for rescue work, but they had a limited load capacity. Then on November 10, 1949, the Sikorsky H-19 made its first flight and proved it could carry 10 passengers and a crew of two more than 350 miles. A military version of the S-55 (which was later certified as a commercial transport aircraft), the H-19 made possible serious consideration of vertical envelopment of battlefields by helicopter-borne troops.

3

Baptism of Fire

Three hours after North Korean armed forces crossed the 38th parallel into South Korea on June 25, 1950, two Sikorsky H-5s of the Air Rescue Service left Tokyo for Seoul, South Korea, carrying American brass to begin organizing resistance.

Before the struggle was over, on July 27, 1953, the helicopter had come of age as a military vehicle, no longer tentatively committed in limited ways as an experimental vessel but deployed as an indispensable battlefield weapon.

There are the usual conflicting claims for the first use of a helicopter on the battlefield—that is, by an American, for the French had used American-made helicopters earlier, in the French Indochina war.

Perhaps the best claim belongs to a Lieutenant Costello of the Third Air Rescue Squadron at Taegu, South Korea. On August 6, 1950, he flew to a medical aid station atop a 3,000-foot mountain. All roads out were cut off by enemy troops. He carried a badly wounded soldier to a field hospital, setting the pattern for a steady stream of battlefield medical evacuations that have been made familiar to tens of millions of television viewers by the program M*A*S*H.

In September, 1950, near Seoul, Maj. Gen. Gerhardt W. Hyatt, the U.S. Army chief of chaplains, witnessed one of the choppers' first medical evacuations. He was a first lieutenant at the time and remembers that all the bystanders knew they were witnessing a gigantic advance in military medicine. As he put it:

"What a thrill it was to see that medevac by helicopter and to realize that here was something which was going to change the whole look of the battlefield.... Before, it would take about 30 minutes to get a wounded man from the battle to a primitive aid station where his condition could be stabilized. Then he would be taken to a regimental aid station for further treatment, and later to a divisional clearing station. At this point, almost a day would have elapsed. At the clearing station, the man's condition would be further stabilized, and then, finally, he could be moved to a field hospital, arriving there two or three days after being wounded."

In the days before the slow-flying helicopter's vulnerability to ground fire and fighter attack had been tested, chopper crews had every right to worry about venturing over battlefields where the enemy was shooting real bullets. Nervous helicopter crews could draw some encouragement from the adventure of Lt. (jg.) Raymond A. Miller and his crewman, R. F. Anderson, who were attacked by three Russian MIGs while evacuating 28 South Korean soldiers trapped behind enemy lines at Changyon, North Korea. The helicopter crew made the delightful discovery that jets could not fly slow enough to hold a well-piloted helicopter in the gunsights.

When the war was only four months old, the U.S. Navy had already recognized the helicopter as the most important development in military machinery of the post-World War II period. An interim evaluation report stated:

"One of the few new tools that has made its presence felt in the Korean War is the helicopter. For broad utility purposes, the helicopter compares somewhat with the appearance of the jeep in the last war."

The navy appraisal pointed out the helicopter's value as a transport between ships, spotting platform for gun control, rescue vehicle behind enemy lines, ambulance, courier, and minefield scout. The report urged the building of helicopter platforms on all suitable ships. It recognized that available craft were primitive in development, but anticipated improvements in newer models. It had taken actual combat to prove to the navy the helicopter's value as a military weapon.

Early in January 1951, Chief Aviation Pilot

The helicopter took over from the navy destroyer the task of picking up pilots who had crashed on takeoff from carriers. One helicopter pilot set some kind of record by picking up Ens. Ben Sutherlin and plopping him back aboard his carrier, the U.S.S. Princeton, *exactly one minute from the time he had catapulted and crashed.*

Duane W. Thorin executed the biggest rescue operation up to that date. Off the coast of North Korea, the Thai frigate H.M.T.S. *Prasae* had run aground in a snowstorm. The 118 officers and men had thrown up earthworks on the beach and were fighting off attacking enemy troops. Thorin spent three days flying through the exchange of small-arms fire, and shuttling between his carrier and the beach, he brought out all hands.

Though Duane W. Thorin is shown here accepting mail for a run from the deck of the U.S.S. *Philippine Sea,* which is a fairly tame enterprise, he is reputed to be the original of the helicopter pilot in James A. Michener's *The Bridges at Toko-ri* who wore a top hat. Mickey Rooney played the role in the movie. Thorin won his legendary role by brilliant and daring use of his machine in the rescue of a whole shipload of Thai sailors cast ashore in enemy territory, plus a dozen other adventures of derring-do. His badge, incidentally, was not a top hat but a baseball cap, as shown here. His chopper crashed on a later volunteer rescue mission, and he spent the rest of the war as a prisoner.

On a later mission, Thorin's luck ran out. He had volunteered to pick up an injured pilot downed in an enemy area so hot with anti-aircraft fire that other helicopters had been driven off. A bad twist of the wind crashed his chopper, and he burned it. Thorin was captured soon after and spent 18 months as a prisoner of war.

Readers of James A. Michener's *The Bridges at Toko-ri* and viewers of the movie will find something reminiscent of Duane Thorin in Michener's helicopter pilot character who affected a top hat during his daring rescue operations; Thorin wore a red baseball cap. The film role was played by Mickey Rooney.

By 1951 helicopter medical evacuation had passed through the improvisation phase and had become big business. During the first three months of operation with the 8055th MASH (Mobile Army Surgical Hospital) unit, three army helicopter detachments with only 11 machines brought out 1,985 wounded, most of them one at a time. A substantial number of the evacuations were made under enemy fire.

After the Red Chinese entered the war and the tide of battle had turned against the American and South Korean forces, helicopter rescue teams performed under ever-more-hazardous conditions. On February 7, 1951, a Mosquito air control light plane flying over the enemy lines spotted a hard-pressed platoon cut off by Communist troops. The pilot called for two Air Rescue Service H-5 helicopters. Flown by Capt. Daniel L. Miller and 1st Lt. Ernest L. MacQuarrie, the choppers followed the plane to the scene, while Mustang fighters circled overhead to discourage interference by the enemy. When the helicopters reached the platoon, the ground troops, huddled in a snow-covered ravine, all appeared dead or unconscious, except for one man who waved feebly.

Captain Miller landed atop a nearby ridge. His medical technician, Corp. John T. Lowe, tried to drag one of the wounded up through the deep snow but collapsed with exhaustion. Miller locked the helicopter controls, left the engine running, and helped the corporal wrestle the soldier aboard. Captain Miller then went down into the snow-filled valley for another casualty. When they were halfway back up the slope, enemy fire became disturbingly accurate and dense, so Miller hid the soldier behind a fold in the ground and ran to his machine to radio for a fighter strafing run.

While he was gone, an aggressive and resourceful wounded soldier had pulled himself into the one empty seat, so Miller took off and dropped his load at a first-aid station 10 miles south.

After the Mustangs worked over the area, Lieutenant MacQuarrie tried to land the other helicopter in a clearing, but the fire was still too hot. Miller came in for a second load and left. MacQuarrie then landed and picked up his quota of two. Miller made the last pickup, but Corporal Lowe had to carry one of the wounded men into the chopper.

In March 1951, a brute of a machine that would enormously expand the helicopter's capabilities arrived in Korea. It was the Sikorsky H-19, capable of carrying 10 passengers and a two-man crew.

The first job for the H-19, in fact the main reason it was rushed over by C-124 Globemaster air transport, was a cloak-and-dagger operation, the theft from under Communist noses of a MIG, the Russian-built jet fighter.

Tantalizingly, a reasonably intact MIG lay where it had been shot down, in a small valley about 35 miles inland from the coast, well beyond the North Korean frontier. Yielding to the intolerable temptation, Gen. Earl E. Partridge, commander of the Fifth Air Force, ordered Capt. Joseph D. Cooper, the H-19 test pilot from Eglin Air Force Base in Florida, to go get it.

On March 19, 1951, Captain Cooper and Capt. Russell Winnegar, the copilot, lifted off with an intelligence officer and six South Korean soldiers to help dismantle the downed craft. Cooper stayed well offshore to avoid detection, landed on a captured North Korean island for refueling, picked up his fighter escort, and flew to the crash site.

Left: Experimental logging by helicopter, begun in 1971, has proved its feasibility and is now spreading, especially in the Pacific Northwest.

Two authentic medevacuation pictures taken during the Korean conflict. Top: A quartet of Marines carry a wounded comrade to a waiting helicopter. Bottom: A helicopter flies a casualty to a field hospital, a scene reproduced before every episode of the television series M★A★S★H.

The H-19 landed about 100 yards from the MIG, and the intelligence spook and his six Korean wreckers fell to. When the dismantling went too slow for the impetuous officer, he blew sections apart with hand grenades. In 45 minutes, they had loaded the MIG into the H-19, with the plane's tail section sticking out into the night wind.

Because the H-19 was overloaded by at least 1,000 pounds, Captain Cooper could not climb out of the valley but had to fly downstream toward a distant gap in the hills, increasing the speed beyond the helicopter's normal limit. Ground batteries harried him the whole long way. Back at the captured island base, the pilot discovered a massive chunk of flak wedged into one of the chopper's rotor blades.

To lighten the load somewhat, the men shifted some parts of the MIG to a little H-5 that had been standing by for rescue work in case the H-19 was shot down. Both helicopters flew to another island, where crews transferred cargo and personnel to an amphibian plane for a flight to Fifth Air Force headquarters. The MIG was rushed aboard an air transport plane bound for the States. Because of the strain of the overload, the H-19 had to be torn down to basic nuts and bolts for an overhaul.

The first naval helicopter carrier in combat was the humble *LST-799*, anchored in Wonsan harbor. At the beginning, the LST-based craft flew freely over captured Wonsan; the enemy waved at passing pilots without apparent rancor. Then just for laughs, some damned fool dropped a hand grenade on an enemy latrine, and the war was on.

Lieutenant T. E. Houston, skipper of the ungainly but serviceable helicopter carrier, reported on the unit's first rescue in April 1951.

"On a beautiful spring afternoon, we had just had emergency rescue drill when the alarm sounded. The boatswain passed the word—'Away the rescue party, away . . . .' Dashing out on deck, I joined the rest of the crew topside watching a parachuting figure whose plane was just crashing into the ocean.

"The LCVP [rescue boat] was away first and the 'copter soon after. But the 'copter reached the downed pilot first, and then as it often happened, the helicopter crewman had to jump into the water and assist the downed pilot into the hoisting sling. While the helicopter returned the pilot, the LCVP picked up the crewman. Except for a chill, both were in good shape.

"This was Ens. M. S. Tuthill's second dunking and second helicopter rescue; he understandably had a high regard for the whirlybirds."

Among the helicopter pilots on the LST was Lt. (jg.) John Kelvin Koelsch, who had completed a full tour of combat rescue duty on the U.S.S. *Princeton,* during which he had invented several lifesaving and safety devices that had been widely adopted by other pilots. He had made at least two rescues. Nevertheless, he had volunteered for a second combat tour.

On July 3, 1951, the helicopter unit was temporarily based on the *LST Q-009*. About an hour before sunset, the radio operator of the LST intercepted a Mayday from a Marine pilot shot down about 40 miles southwest of Wonsan. Lieutenant Koelsch and his crewman, George M. Neal, volunteered for the mission, despite the impending darkness and worsening weather. Escorted by four Corsair fighters, the chopper reached the rescue site and plunged through the cloud cover. A few minutes later, the pilots of the fighter planes heard Koelsch report that he had found the Marine and was going down. Because the site was in the Anbyon Valley, the enemy's main supply route in the area, it bristled with anti-aircraft weapons. The Corsair pilots worried about the helicopter—and with good reason, for they heard no more from Lieutenant Koelsch.

Captain James V. Wilkins, the downed Marine, told the story of his attempted rescue after his release from prison camp at war's end— "He found me, after two passes into the most intense small-arms fire I've ever witnessed," the captain began.

Wilkins climbed into the sling just as a burst

The first service to understand the potential of the helicopter in combat was the U.S. Marine Corps. In Korea the Marines pushed into mountainous regions beyond the reach of normal infantry operations, counting on the helicopter to supply, reinforce, and evacuate. Here on May 23, 1951, Marines send out their wounded from atop Kari San Mountain.

of fire hit the helicopter, and it smashed into the mountainside. The air crew scrambled out unhurt, but Wilkins suffered badly burned legs. For nine days, Lieutenant Koelsch and Neal miraculously avoided capture while carrying Wilkins on a crude pallet. On July 12, they reached the beach, and their spirits lifted. Hunger finally drove Koelsch to risk trying to steal or beg food from a nearby village. Soon after, the trio was captured. After a few months in prison camp, Koelsch died of starvation and dysentery.

For his heroism in the attempted rescue, his long walk to the beach with his wounded comrade, and his courage and leadership during captivity, on August 3, 1955, Lieutenant Koelsch was awarded posthumously the Congressional Medal of Honor. The record makes no mention of the gallant airman George Neal.

Though they had been pressed into rescue service, the navy's Wonsan-based helicopters originally had been sent out as minesweeping auxiliaries. They scouted ahead of the surface minesweepers. When they spotted floating mines, they punctured them with rifle fire till the day one exploded and touched off four more by sympathetic shock, almost knocking the chopper from the air.

Like the helicopters that had conned the icebreakers of Operation High Jump through leads in the ice, the Wonsan choppers often guided minesweepers through minefields in which the

ships were trapped. The helicopters traced out the cleared channels, much easier to spot from the air than from the water's surface.

Because the Korean War was an international effort—token forces from 15 nations fought alongside the South Koreans and Americans—military services of other countries were also involved in helicopter missions. On October 20, 1951, for instance, the skipper of the Australian ship H.M.A.S. *Sydney* received a message that a Firefly plane and two airmen were down near Sasiwan, in North Korea. Although it was nearly sunset and regulations forbade after-dark helicopter missions, Chief Aviation Pilot A. K. Babbitt and his crewman, an airman named Gooding, volunteered to go after the downed fliers. Two Sea Fury fighters flew cover.

At the scene, the helicopter crew still had enough light to see Communist troops closing in on the downed fliers, who were trying to hold them off with their light weapons. The Sea Furies strafed the area, and Gooding sprayed the attackers with a submachine gun from the helicopter door. The helicopter set down only 20 feet from the crash victims, and Gooding jumped out to help them, still clutching his submachine gun.

Seeing the chopper on the ground as a possible prize, the enemy charged. Gooding mowed them down while the Australian fliers boarded the helicopter. Covering his retreat with machine-gun fire, Gooding climbed in, and the craft sped to Kimp'o airfield, where headlights from a line of jeeps marked the landing strip. The rescue won Babbitt the Navy Cross, and Gooding the Commendation Ribbon with Distinguishing Device, indicating it was earned in combat.

Equipped with the powerful new H-19, the Marines tested their vertical-envelopment theory on the battlefield. Between September and December 1951, they moved hundreds of leathernecks about the front by vertical lift. The Fleet Marine Force Air Evaluation Report said, "The goal of long-range Marine Corps planning for employment of this vehicle in amphibious assault was advanced significantly . . . when, for the first time in history, the helicopter was used to deploy large numbers of troops into combat."

The Marines also mounted Operation Ripple, a maneuver in which a fleet of helicopters flew rockets, rocket launchers, and crews to a firing site, stood by while the crews launched a ripple of rockets, and then rushed men and equipment to another firing site—all of this to foil counterbattery fire. Although the operation seems like a tremendous effort for a small effect, the Marine report declared the tactic "feasible."

As the war ground on, the Marines seized every chance to develop their vertical-envelopment tactic. In one engagement, they lifted by

---

Helicopter crewmen suffered some freakish accidents. As he was leaving the front lines, Col. T. A. Culhane, Jr., commanding the Fifth Marine Regiment, had trouble getting his helicopter off and away. While he was hovering a few feet off the ground, fighting for lift-off, a shell burst under his craft and punched the helicopter into a soaring climb. The next two rounds of enemy shells obliterated the takeoff site the colonel had just left.

H-19 an entire battalion to the top of Mountain 884 and kept it supplied. (The assault plan bore the excruciatingly cute name of Operation Changie Changie.) Eventually, the Marines routinely crossed rivers by helicopter. They soon discovered they could move more Koreans because they were smaller than Americans.

The Marines' Third Evaluation Report complained, however, that winds through narrow defiles created such turbulence that often even the H-19 could not make forward flight. Payloads were cut below the manufacturer's recommendations, so that instead of the 10-man combat unit the craft was designed to carry, the helicopter lifted only six Koreans or five Americans. In hot weather, when the rotors took a weaker bite of air, helicopters sometimes could lift only four Americans.

Worried about slow helicopter takeoffs on the battlefield, military theoreticians decided to try the jet-assisted takeoffs (JATO) that had successfully boosted fixed-wing aircraft off short runways. At the Patuxent, Maryland, flight test headquarters, authorities called for volunteers to test a Sikorsky HO4S with a JATO tube mounted vertically in the bottom of the cabin. Nobody stepped forward, so Lt. Comdr. Ed Arnold drew the dubious job.

After the JATO bottle blasted the helicopter into the air, it was supposed to drop clear. The schedule called for 12 test takeoffs, and the first 11 went well. But the staff wanted to rush the tests through so they could get the JATO bottles shipped to Korea and off the premises.

On January 5, 1952, Lieutenant Commander Arnold rolled out the HO4S, even though it was a Saturday and supposedly a day off. No other fliers were around to fill the copilot seat, so Arnold called Lt. Col. Armand DeLalio at home and asked him to help get the JATO test program finished once and for all. DeLalio was a famed helicopter pioneer and agreed to assist in a vertical-flight experiment one more time.

On takeoff the JATO bottle sputtered and

started to drop from the tube, then it hung up, fired again, and shot through the craft, cutting fuel lines and controls. The helicopter crashed and burned, killing both pilots.

Back in Korea, the chopper pilot's principal hazard in front-line evacuation missions was dense small-arms fire, but the army's official report described a more sophisticated threat: ". . . The most dreaded of enemy anti-aircraft guns were the 85-mm. radar-controlled weapons. They were uncannily accurate with their anti-aircraft fire. If you flew at 8,215 feet, that's where the first bursts were."

As in the encounters with jet fighters, the helicopter's very weakness turned out to be its best defense against the 85-mm. guns. The craft flew so slow that the deadly cannon invariably drew too long a lead. By no means did all helicopters escape the anti-aircraft shells, but as the army report put it, "Thank God they usually misjudged our speed."

Fighter planes and bombers were the prime

Private First Class Gene A. Thaxton won the kind of honor most soldiers would just as soon forego. Critically wounded on a mountain slope, he was carried to a front-line aid station, given whole blood, and loaded into an H-13 flown by Capt. Hubert D. Gaddis. He arrived at a MASH unit with the distinction of being the 10,000th medical evacuation of the war.

targets of the big guns, and many behind-the-lines helicopter missions were made to pick up fixed-wing pilots downed by anti-aircraft fire. A typical rescue was that of Robert E. Galer, a Marine colonel and a Congressional Medal of Honor winner in World War II. (He had been shot down four times while downing 11 Japanese planes at Guadalcanal to win his medal.)

On June 10, 1952, with the help of helicopters

One of the most tragic accidents in helicopter history. On January 5, 1952, two famous pioneer rotary-wing pilots took off in this HO4S, lifted aloft on a rocket in an experiment to help overloaded helicopters take off quickly on the Korean front. The rocket blew through the cabin, severing fuel lines and controls. Lieutenant Commander Ed Arnold and Lt. Col. Armand DeLalio died in the crash.

based on the *LST-799*, Colonel Galer cheated death for the fifth time. As he pulled out of a bomb run far behind enemy lines in Korea, his Corsair caught a burst of 37-mm. flak that carved away the leading edge of one wing and the engine mount. He struggled to regain friendly territory, but the plane could not make it. Galer jumped to bail out, his foot caught on a strap inside the cockpit. The one-time All-American basketball player had strength enough to fight his way against the buffeting wind back into the cockpit to free his foot. As he cleared the plane, the tail struck him a stunning blow in the side and shoulder.

"I estimate the chute opened about 150 feet from the ground," Colonel Galer later reported. "I floated down through the smoke of the crash and landed within 10 feet of the wreckage. The plane was burning, and some of the ammo was exploding. While getting out of my chute, I heard small-arms fire."

Colonel Galer had several broken ribs and an injured shoulder and left arm, but his legs carried him to cover on a steep slope. He waited while three enemy soldiers searched the wrecked Corsair. When they gave up and drifted off, he signaled for help.

The *LST-799* received Galer's Mayday about 5:00 P.M., shortly before sunset. The rescue action report follows:

"There was a pilot down about 60 miles in a straight line southwest of Wonsan.... This 120-mile round trip was just about maximum for a rescue helicopter. It was also very late in the afternoon, and there was doubt that enough daylight remained to effect a rescue. Flight after sunset was extremely difficult because the horizon was often not visible. Moreover, the flight had to be made over a circuitous route to skirt known gun positions. And to make the rescue even more ticklish, the rescue would be made at a height near the helicopter's ceiling. It was decided to give it a try."

The pilot was Lt. (jg.) H. O. McEachern, and

his crewman was Ted J. Lee. They flew an HO3S. The report continues:

"Along the way, the helicopter ran into seven anti-aircraft positions in only 35 miles. At the rescue site, a Corsair ... directed the helicopter pilot to Colonel Galer, who set off a smoke flare. He was on a 45-degree slope."

"I came to a hover," Lieutenant McEachern reported, "while my crewman, Ted Lee, let out the full length of the hoist line. I had to increase power [to] maximum. At this point, the pilot was in the sling. I could no longer hold my position and let the plane fall down into the valley ..."

The helicopter's drift dragged Colonel Galer through the brush, but he clung to the hoist. McEachern recovered control and lifted clear. Crewman Lee pulled Galer into the cabin.

Both chopper and fighter escort were low on fuel, so they had to fly a direct route over known anti-aircraft positions. The route seemed "full of red floating balls and smoke puffs." Lee jettisoned any gear they could spare. When they reached the coast, the *LST-799* turned on its navigational lights, a horrifying experience for sailors in wartime. The helicopter engine coughed ominously but resumed its reassuring chop. The craft landed at about 9:00 P.M., with only seconds of fuel left. The rescue mission earned McEachern the Navy Cross and Lee the Silver Star.

Not all such rescue efforts were successful, but many helicopter crews who failed in their missions were more fortunate than the Koelsch-Neal team, whose attempt ended so tragically. On a Friday the 13th, Capt. Jack Schmidt and Corp. Robert Sarvia volunteered to go after a Mustang pilot who had parachuted 20 miles behind enemy lines in the mountains north of Kwachon Reservoir. Mustangs and Corsairs escorted the chopper.

Immediately over the jump site, small-arms fire brought down the helicopter. Sarvia suffered a badly twisted leg. The Mustang pilot, Maj. Bryce McIntyre, who had a dislocated shoulder, joined the helicopter crew, and the trio took cover from the Communists' fire. The fighter escort held back the enemy while another helicopter, piloted by Capt. Frank E. Wilson, flew up from the base.

Because of the enemy fire, Captain Schmidt tried to wave off his own rescue, but Wilson bored through. The ground was too rough for a landing, so Wilson hovered while Sarvia climbed into the rescue sling. An air current shot the helicopter 150 feet straight up with Sarvia swinging below. The injured airman fought his way up to the door but could not make it over the sill. Wilson pulled him in by the collar; no small feat, for flying a helicopter in tricky wind currents requires at least two hands.

Captain Wilson returned and picked up the other two but could not take off because their weight unbalanced the chopper. With bullets swarming all around, Schmidt jumped out while Wilson redistributed sandbags to trim his craft. Schmidt then climbed aboard and the helicopter lifted off. The overloaded craft staggered down the canyon. In the gathering dusk, machine-gun tracers stitched the air all about. The fighter escort pasted enemy gun positions with napalm and rockets, knocking out one 40-mm. and four 20-mm. batteries. Improvised flare pots and jeep and truck headlights illuminated the field for the night landing.

In another rescue effort, three helicopter crews were called in before the mission was accomplished. Late in March 1952, Ens. Harlo E. Sterrett, Jr., fighter pilot from the U.S.S. *Valley Forge*, bailed out of his Corsair and landed on a 6,200-foot-high plateau deep in North Korea. His squadron mates flew cover while light planes dropped "survival bombs" containing guns, ammunition, food, and a short-wave radio. The light helicopter from the cruiser U.S.S. *Saint Paul* that flew in to pick up Sterrett was driven off by turbulence, so Rear Adm. John Perry, commanding Task Force 77, ordered up a heavier helicopter, the Marines' HRS-1. Darkness fell before the chopper could take off.

On the second day, Ensign Sterrett's squadron mate and close friend, Ens. Roland G. Busch,

crashed and died while trying to relocate the downed pilot.

The following morning, Maj. Dwain E. Lengel, Capt. Eugene V. Pointer, and T. Sgt. C. E. Gricks took off from the U.S.S. *Valley Forge* in an HRS-1, escorted by four Corsairs and one Skyraider. A mile from the point where Sterrett had last been seen, a downdraft slammed the helicopter to the ground. Nobody was hurt, so the crew stripped the wrecked aircraft of movable gear, and the fighters strafed the hulk till it caught fire.

Rain closed down operations for two days, with the rescue crew isolated behind enemy lines.

Another HRS-1, stripped of all excess weight including a fuel reserve, came in to pick up the downed rescuers. It was flown by Capt. Robert J. Lesak and 1st Lt. "Wes" Wessel. Corsairs escorted the helicopter.

Reluctant to get too close to the rocky surface of the treacherous plateau, Lesak and Wessel made a slow pass dragging a 40-foot rope ladder. Sergeant Gricks dropped his boots and carbine, grabbed the ladder, and fought his way up against the rotor blast. The pilot had to make three more passes before Captain Pointer caught the ladder, but he was too weak from overexertion at the high altitude to climb all the way. He was hanging outside when shots rang out from surrounding hills. The Corsairs tore up the enemy nest. None of the Marines were hit.

The helicopter's fuel was beginning to run low, so when Major Lengel missed the ladder on the first run, he told the pilot over his walkie-talkie to give up. Captain Lesak answered, "Negative, Major. I'm making another run for you."

Lengel caught the last rung and dangled by his arms as the overloaded helicopter skimmed over the treetops, fighting to gain altitude. Meanwhile, Captain Pointer was helped into the cabin. Lengel finally got one leg over a rung and finished the laborious climb into the chopper as it flew off to the U.S.S. *Saint Paul*.

Ensign Sterrett was later picked up by a Wonsan-based LST carrier helicopter flown by

Lt. C. R. Severns and crewman T. C. Roche.

The tape of an LST-based chopper rescue has survived and gives one the feeling of a routine behind-the-lines mission. Aboard *LST-735* near Wonsan, Lt. Comdr. Donald L. Good and his crewman, Theodore R. Smith, took off in an HO3S to pick up the pilot of an Air Force Sabre jet who had jumped to a snow-covered hillside. Over the site, Good picked up two jet fighters from the Rescue Combat Air Patrol—RESCAP, in military parlance. Their radio exchange follows:

RESCAP: The downed pilot has to stay low to avoid heavy small-arms fire.
  Good: This is Angel Five...I have chute in sight...We are under heavy fire... Can pilot get in the open?
RESCAP: This is RESCAP. Follow the two planes ahead of you. I will strafe trenches.
  Smith: Mr. Good, they're shooting at us; one hit back here.
  Good: That's their prerogative. This is Angel Five, I have chute in sight...We are under heavy fire...Can you get pilot in open?
RESCAP: This is RESCAP. We will strafe for you...Pilot reports hip-deep snow prevents his getting into the open.
  Good: This is Angel Five. I see him now... It's a bad place, but will try...May be able to pick him up on the run.
         (*Silence—except for planes on strafing runs*)
  Smith: He's in the sling now, Mr. Good, coming up.
RESCAP: This is RESCAP. The chopper got the pilot. Come on, boys, let's go down and strafe ahead. He's almost over the water now.
         (*At this time a flight of eight navy planes arrived over Wonsan harbor*)
  Dumbo: Can we help?

RESCAP: You bet...Strafe hell out of Wonsan as he comes out.
  Dumbo: Roger...This is Dumbo...The chopper is over the water now...I'll escort him back to ship.

Nobody really knows how many medical evacuations were chalked up during the Korean conflict, but it was in five figures. Before Korea up to 90 percent of the combat casualties suffering head or stomach wounds died. In Korea quick evacuation by helicopter cut the figure to 10 percent.

When the Communists agreed to truce talks, Gen. Matthew B. Ridgway sent United Nations delegates to the conferences in helicopters instead of jeeps. Ridgway suspected that the North Koreans would photograph the white flags on the ground vehicles for propaganda purposes, using the pictures to prove that the Allies were surrendering.

The Far East navy commander's headquarters issued the following appreciation of the helicopter's first combat experience:

"If any single aircraft type ever sold itself...

Even in so grim a task as medical evacuation, Americans can invent a way to make a sporting competition out of it. Late in 1951, 1st Lt. Joseph L. Bowler, one of two pilots who had made the first army medical evacuations in Korea, achieved his 824th evacuation (in 482 missions), to set the Korean—that is to say, the world's—record. An old friend and rival, Lt. William P. Brake, arrived in Korea a year later and swore to break the record. He had to extend his combat tour in order to do it, but he flew his 825th evacuation (in 545 missions) on April 22, 1953. He wanted to try for 1,000 but settled for a prodigious record of 900 evacuations before going home on May 14, 1953.

Ensign E. H. Barry, trying to escape his ditched Grumman Guardian alongside the U.S.S. *Block Island* on August 12, 1953, was almost done in by an overdose of safety devices. The rescue helicopter got him into the sling and on his way up when his opened parachute snatched him loose and pulled him back into the water. He finally freed himself from his chute and made it to the helicopter.

it is the helicopter . . . . When the UN forces began their rapid counterattack to the north, the fleet was called upon for close support and interdiction firing. The helicopter became the eyes of the fleet and was primarily responsible for accurate and devastating fire . . . . In land-rescue operations, the helicopter proved itself time and again. Many of our lads owe their lives to its land and sea rescue capabilities."

Prophetically, the report concluded, "In another war, all commands will be asking for larger numbers of helicopters."

4

In Peaceful Service

Even though virtually all the money for helicopter development came from the military, the civilian world grasped the machine's potential more quickly than the armed services.

As early as 1947, several police departments, led by New York City's, patrolled with helicopters. The Los Angeles County sheriff even mounted kennels on the sides of his helicopters so he could rush bloodhounds into remote areas to track criminals or lost children. Many houses and stores installed 1,000-watt beacons on their rooftops as burglar alarms to attract police helicopters when intruders tripped the switch. The police helicopters would hover over the burglarized building with floodlights blazing to prevent escape of the intruder.

Having exhausted the possibilities of finding new, easily worked petroleum fields on solid land, the oil industry extended its operations offshore at just about the time the indispensable offshore tool, the helicopter, had evolved far enough to support the move.

Now a giant that dominates the commercial helicopter world, Petroleum Helicopters, Incorporated, of Lafayette and New Orleans, Louisiana, entered the field in 1949 by offering the services of three Bell 47-D helicopters to the companies searching for oil in the coastal marshes and offshore shelves of Louisiana.

One of the first of Petroleum's pilots, L. L. (Red) McCombie, recounted an episode that may

have led to the litter evacuation technique which later saved thousands of lives in Korea.

"I went into the marsh late one afternoon to bring out a couple of seismic crewmen. My battery blew up and stranded me along with them. Because we hadn't planned on spending the night in the marsh, we didn't have a mosquito net or repellent. We didn't relish coating ourselves with mud to escape the mosquitoes, so I lit a flare and hoped somebody would see it. Another helicopter pilot did spot the light and came after us.

"A Bell 47-D had only one passenger seat, so we gave the oldest one of us the place of honor because of his seniority. Slim and I straddled a float on each side and hung on. I was hoping Slim was strong so he could hang on the whole 10 miles across White Lake. If he fell off, I would have to jump to save the other two because the craft would turn over under the unbalanced weight.

"In the glow of the hot exhaust pipe, I could see Slim's teeth flashing, so I figured he was grinning and everything was okay. Anyway, we made it fine and proved the Bell 47-D could do it."

When federal officials wanted a male whooping crane from the Gulf Coast marshes for an experimental breeding program designed to save the species from extinction, even the most experienced bogtrotters could not run down the fleet-footed bird. McCombie did the job, by chasing one with his Bell helicopter till the crane keeled over from exhaustion and submitted to capture.

This extraordinary photograph shows the actual rescue of a missing child, who has collapsed on a mountainside. The craft is a Bell 47G of the Los Angeles County Sheriff's Department.

Carrying a load of Thanksgiving turkeys to American troops in Europe, in 1952, the S.S. *Grommet Reefer* went aground and broke in two in the harbor at Leghorn, Italy, within sight of the Italian Naval Academy. Crews of other ships nearby, using highline and small boats, made slow going of the rescue. The cadets managed to send the accumulated personal mail to the shipwrecked sailors. The U.S. Navy, with a different set of priorities, rushed in helicopters to lift out the rest of the merchant ship's crew.

Its lifesaving techniques honed in Korea, the helicopter was now in demand for rescue work all over the globe. Late in 1952, the S.S. *Grommet Reefer*, a refrigeration ship under contract to carry turkeys for American troops in Austria, crashed into rocks in the harbor at Leghorn, Italy. The ship broke in two, the stern section lodging only 200 yards offshore from the Italian Naval Academy. The bow section sank, but the entire ship's company had already taken refuge on the stern. Crews from the ships of Air Repair Division Two, in Leghorn at the time, began the rescue operation, using highline and small boats. Winds blowing at up to 60 knots gave them a hard workout, and after several hours only three of the shipwrecked sailors had been brought ashore. The

Italian cadets from the academy, who had flocked to the beach for a practical lesson in sea rescue, bolstered morale aboard the threatened craft by sending the sailors via highline their mail that had accumulated in the Leghorn post office.

Fearing that the stern would break up in the high seas before all the ship's crew could be saved, Vice Adm. John Cassaday, commander of the Sixth Fleet, rushed Carrier Division Four to the scene. Four helicopters from the U.S.S. *Midway*, the *Pittsburgh*, and the *Leyte* flew in to assist in the rescue, hovering over the wreck. Crewman P. Teitmeyer lowered himself to the deck so he could show the sailors how to use the rescue sling. One hour and 45 minutes after the choppers arrived, all 39 of the merchant ship's crew had

Despite its poor technical quality, this picture dramatically shows the last-minute rescue possibilities of the helicopter. This Sikorsky S-55 minutes earlier had lifted two survivors of the storm-wrecked *Laurie* after they had clung to the rigging for seven hours. The machine belonged to the New Orleans Coast Guard station. The *Laurie* went down in the Gulf of Mexico 40 miles southeast of New Orleans.

been saved. (The descent of Teitmeyer to the ship's deck was neither foolhardy nor unnecessary, for many rescue helicopters in the early days were hampered by deckhands who, perhaps afraid the helicopters would run away, would unhook litters and slings and snap the hoist hooks to the ship's stanchions.)

Rescue helicopters kept busy in Canada also. In 1952 the lighthouse keeper at St. Paul Island in Cabot Strait, northeast of Nova Scotia, suffered a fractured skull and broken arm in a dynamite explosion. Lieutenant W. E. James flew his helicopter to Sydney, Nova Scotia, picked up a doctor, and bored through gale winds to the lighthouse. He landed in a snow squall, so he kept the rotors turning to prevent a snow buildup on the blades. Within 45 minutes, the doctor had prepared the patient for evacuation, and the craft took off for the mainland. Lieutenant James won the Most Excellent Order of the British Empire.

Only a few days later, a helicopter rushed two little girls who had been hurt in a sledding accident to Halifax, Nova Scotia, for brain surgery. With its almost gentle takeoff and landing, the helicopter is the ideal vehicle for moving patients with serious head injuries.

When a Canadian Sea Fury fighter plane crashed in the brush near Shearwater Station in Dartmouth, Nova Scotia, a Sikorsky HO4S hovered while its copilot, Lt. D. A. Muncaster, lowered

Sir Edmund Hillary, first conqueror of Mount Everest, used a Bell 47G-3 to rush to the outside world what he believed to be the scalp of an Abominable Snowman. Unfortunately, experts ruled that the eminent explorer had been taken in and his gift to science was not what he thought it was.

himself to the ground. The plane was burning, and the pilot was trapped in the cockpit, so Muncaster bashed his way through the plastic canopy with his fists. He dragged out the pilot just before the fuel tanks exploded and the craft was engulfed in flames. Lieutenant Muncaster received the George Cross in a ceremony at Buckingham Palace in London.

Back in this country, the U.S. Coast Guard, which had made the first practical use of the vertical-lift craft, began pressing for the replace-

By 1950 helicopters were regularly being used to clean up fairgrounds by blowing trash into a central collection tent.

Dwight D. Eisenhower, the first pilot to become president, learned to fly an airplane and received his license when he was stationed in the Philippines before World War II. He was also the first president with a helicopter at his disposal. Here his chopper takes off from the South Lawn of the White House. Today a fleet of helicopters serves the White House.

ment of amphibious rescue planes by helicopters.

On February 22, 1953, a Coast Guard helicopter, piloted by Lt. Comdr. Robert Eastman, with Jack Halsey as crewman and hoist operator, took off to rescue seven men on a cabin cruiser being swamped by heavy surf off Fleischbacker Beach in San Francisco, California. Eastman made four passes over the boat, trailing the sling, but the boat was heaving 20 feet on each swell, and none of the men could catch the sling. The boat broached, broke in two, and sank. Five men swam free, but the other two floated face downward.

The conscious swimmers did not grasp the idea that they were supposed to pass the sling over their heads and under their arms. They just clamped their hands around the loop and hung on while Halsey sweated out the pickup, fearing they would fall back into the sea.

After Eastman had picked up four of the seven men, the combined weight of the six in the chopper forced him to fly to the beach and unload.

On the second effort, he picked up a fifth survivor, but by this time the two bodies floating face downward had disappeared.

This rescue was one of many that pointed up the shortcomings of the horsecollar sling. Shortly afterward, a woman being picked up from a sinking ship fell to her death from a horsecollar. The Coast Guard soon replaced them with rescue baskets, but other services retained the unreliable sling.

Although the Coast Guard was principally animated by the lifesaving spirit, it was, after all, a branch of the Treasury Department (until 1966, that is). So T-men often pressed Coast Guard helicopters into service to sniff out tax evaders. In a single flight, for example, one helicopter found 12 stills that were cheating the government out of $4,000 daily.

Two hurricanes in one week caused disastrous flooding in New England in 1955. Helicopter factories pressed into service machines finished for the armed services but not yet delivered. This Kaman HOK-1, built for the Marines and flown by Kaman's chief test pilot, Al Newton, is hoisting a victim from the rooftop of a flooded building. The electric hoist was only partly available at the time, and many pilots had to improvise lifts; one tied an auto tire to his rope.

Increasingly, helicopters were performing mass rescue missions in natural disasters and major medical emergencies. When the worst earthquakes in Greek history shook the Ionian Islands, killing hundreds, the U.S.S. *Franklin D. Roosevelt* acted as a refueling base for U.S. Army, Navy, and Air Force helicopters, as well as those of Greece. In three days, the choppers flew 90 missions into the mountains where the survivors had fled. Pilots dropped notes written in Greek to isolated groups huddled in the hills, telling them where to find emergency medical stations and soup kitchens. The helicopters carried in 200 tons of food and medical supplies to keep the emergency stations running.

In June 1954, in one of the navy's worst peacetime disasters, two HO4S helicopters, piloted by Lts. Thomas G. Condon and Richard M. Underwood, shuttled between the U.S.S. *Bennington* and the naval hospital at Newport, Rhode Island, carrying 34 badly burned victims of a shipboard explosion that killed more than 100.

Nature struck a blow at New England on August 6, 1955, when Hurricane Carol, followed five days later by Hurricane Diane, ravaged the northeast coast. Early reports placed the dead at 60, most of them children.

Helicopters gathered from all over the eastern seaboard. The National Guard flew in 16, the U.S. Navy another 16, the First Army two, and one each from West Point and the U.S. Marines. The Kaman helicopter factory supplied two, the Sikorsky plant furnished all their completed but undelivered craft.

Kaman's chief test pilot, Al Newton, flew a helicopter unequipped with a hoist. Hovering over

A chopper searches a Connecticut village for victims of floods caused by hurricanes Carol and Diane.

a family of nine, including four children, trapped in an attic, he lowered a bare rope—all he had to offer. (Another pilot tied an auto tire to his rope.) A woman clutching her smallest child grabbed the end of the swinging cable and managed to hang on while she was transported to dry land.

"I don't know how she felt, dangling 300 feet above the ground," Newton said, "but I know I was scared stiff I'd let them hit a high-tension line."

Miraculously, he got the whole family out without dropping anybody. When hoist-equipped helicopters arrived, however, Newton decided he had strained his luck far enough and switched to carrying medical supplies and doctors.

Another Kaman test pilot, Pete Russell, was attracted to a flooded backyard in Bloomfield, Connecticut, by a lone figure waving a beach umbrella to catch his attention. Turned out to be the aptly named Dr. Howard J. Wetstone, who was volunteering for duty.

One Sikorsky helicopter, piloted by Lt. Giuseppe Bello of the navy, with Richard Colver as copilot, alone picked up 200 refugees. Another Sikorsky, that was to be delivered to the Royal Canadian Air Force and already marked with the RCAF insignia, was rejected by an old lady who feared the unfamiliar escutcheon signaled a Russian invasion.

In California the same year, floods engulfed whole communities. Lieutenant Command-

In October 1955, a killer hurricane struck Tampico, Mexico. The major rescue effort was by helicopters based on the carriers U.S.S. *Siboney* and U.S.S. *Saipan.* Here a helicopter is lifting an entire family from a rooftop. The choppers rescued 5,500 people.

On July 25, 1956, the S.S. *Stockholm* and the S.S. *Andrea Doria* unaccountably collided in the Atlantic, about 50 miles from Nantucket Island, despite the supposed security offered by modern navigational safeguards such as radar. The *Andrea Doria* sank with great loss of life. The *Stockholm* survived. Here a U.S. Coast Guard HO4S is lifting injured victims of the collision from the fantail of the *Stockholm*.

er George Thometz and Lt. Henry Pfeiffer of the Coast Guard flew without rest for 15 hours to make 138 rescues, 58 of them at night. Pfeiffer developed a tactic of chopping off annoying television antennas with his rotor and blowing them away with the downblast. Both pilots won the Distinguished Flying Cross.

That same disastrous year of 1955, a hurricane killed hundreds in Tampico, Mexico. The U.S. Navy sent the helicopter carriers U.S.S. *Saipan* and U.S.S. *Siboney*, a helicopter training squadron from Pensacola, Florida, a Marine helicopter group, and two Marine fixed-wing transport squadrons to the scene. The choppers picked up 5,500 Mexicans marooned on roofs, trees, and telephone poles and delivered 183,000 pounds of food and medical supplies. The rescue effort prompted a great flurry of diplomatic documents to express the Mexican republic's gratitude.

During 1955 also, the Liberian freighter *Kismet II* smashed into the rocks at the base of a 1,000-foot cliff on Canada's Cape Breton Island. A Canadian Navy helicopter, manned by Lt.

In the mid-1950s, the New York Trap Rock Company began distributing paychecks by helicopter to barge crews scattered about the Hudson River and New York Harbor.

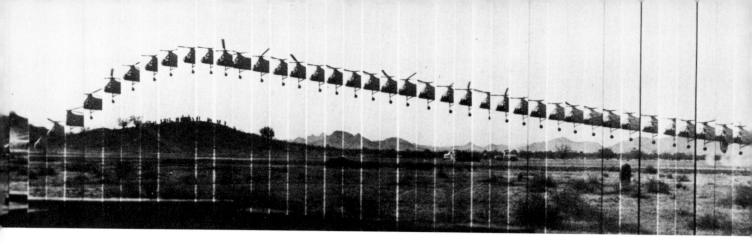

A Kaman helicopter drone demonstrates pilotless controlled flight. The program was developed to provide the U.S. Navy with an antisubmarine device.

Patrol of power lines today is routinely done by helicopters flying low and slow or even by not flying at all but hovering while the inspector takes a long, close look at a possible trouble spot.

Comdr. Jack H. Beeman, copilot Roger Fink, and crewmen L. P. Vipond and P. A. Smith, made seven tries to hover over the doomed ship, but winds gusting to 80 knots, the looming cliff, and gathering darkness drove them off. The next morning, Beeman and his crew returned and by hand signals instructed the stranded seamen to tear away rails, the binnacle, masts, and other superstructure to clear a landing spot. Beeman made four landings on the cleared deck, carrying out 21 sailors, the ship's cat, and the captain's dog. Queen Elizabeth II awarded the George Cross to the two officers and the Queen's Commendation to the crewmen.

When Seaman Steven W. Patryn was seriously injured on the destroyer U.S.S. *Hazelwood* off Newport, Rhode Island, in 1956, a heavy fog prevented a manned emergency flight. The U.S. Navy was still experimenting with unmanned, antisubmarine helicopters, run by remote control—called the DASH system, an acronym for Drone Anti-Submarine Helicopter—so the commanding officer, Comdr. Harry Snyder, authorized a DASH flight. The pilot, Ralph Lee, took off from the ship with his patient and trimmed for level flight, then turned over control to Lt. James Julian, who flew the helicopter through the fog by remote control from the ship's radar center. When the craft broke out of the fog over the mainland, Lee took back control and landed at the Naval Underwater Ordnance Station, where his patient was transferred to an ambulance.

Meanwhile, all kinds of odd jobs were turning up for the helicopter pilot, many of them too hazardous or literally impossible for any other craft to tackle. Down under, Australia's island-state, Tasmania, suffered its worst freeze in years

Left: A Hiller 12E reels out a thick transmission line from a gigantic spool to string it across a 17-pole span, doing the job in 24 minutes as opposed to eight hours by conventional means.
Right: A lineman directs the pilot in positioning the wire on the pole. The helicopter operation saved the Union Electric Company of St. Louis, Missouri, 36 percent in line-stringing costs.

in August 1956. Ice broke the northwest coast power line, and the highlands lay under snow too deep for a land patrol to locate the break. Australian National Airways had just bought a British-built Bristol Sycamore helicopter and had given it the jawbreaking name of Yarranana. Although roads were closed and icing conditions too dangerous for fixed-wing craft, Capt. Max Holyman, the Sycamore's pilot, allowed he would "give it a go." With two engineers, he left Hobart to patrol the power line, looking for the break. Holyman tells about the flight.

"Snow was falling very heavily, and the wind gusting up to 70 miles per hour. The turbulence was severe, but at no time did I have any concern for the performance or safety of the helicopter. After 50 minutes of struggling, we came across the power line and pinpointed ourselves.

"Visibility at this stage was getting as low as 50 yards, not because of snow falling but due to the strong wind whipping up the stuff which had already come down and was lying deep on the

ground. It was whipped to 30 feet up, obliterating the power line and towers. It became difficult at times to say whether you were flying above the snow on the ground or above one of those localized blizzards. We . . . crabbed north. We flew along the line at an average height of 20 feet. After 20 minutes of struggling, the break in the line was sighted. We landed at the power plant and told the engineers where the break was. They sent a ground team."

The same year, a New Zealand pilot marked a frightening first by taking a Bell 47-G inside the caldera of a live volcano to set up a geophone. He made repeated trips to the 7,515-foot summit and dipped into a cloud of steam to transport geophone housing, apparatus, and pre-mixed concrete. He then laid three-quarters of a mile of cable to a point where ground crews could safely connect it to the main cable.

But for weird cable-laying jobs, Kern Copters, Incorporated, took the prize in 1957. (Kern has since gone out of business.)

Pilot Charles E. Green, Jr., laying a cable from the South Rim of the Grand Canyon to the canyon floor for construction of a tramway to lift bat guano from a cave 600 feet up the canyon wall. (Cave is at right in picture at right.) The cable was paid out from a reel specially designed for the job. Green's biggest danger in the near-vertical descent was that the reel would jam and draw cable into the rotors. The job took 2½ minutes and went without a hitch.

Kern's project was to string 11,500 feet of 1/8th-inch cable from the top of the South Rim of the Grand Canyon to the canyon floor on the north side of the Colorado River, a plunge of 3,000 feet. This cable would be used to draw successively heavier lines across the canyon to make up a permanent 1½-inch cable which, suspended on steel towers, would support a tramway hoist.

To hoist what?

Bat guano.

According to local legend, a teenager poking about the canyon in the 1930s had discovered a 60-million-year-old cave, 600 feet above the river on the canyon wall. The cave was crammed with 100,000 tons of guano, dropped by untold millions of prehistoric bats. The boy supposedly sold his claim for $50, though the deposits, used for fertilizer, have been valued at $10 million. The owners in 1957, the United States Guano Company, had tried to barge the guano but were foiled by the river's sandbars and swift currents. In 1954

they had hired a helicopter pilot to lift it out in a sling, 400 pounds at a time. Too expensive. The company finally decided to build a tramway—but how to lay the cable across that vast hole?

"We considered using weather balloons, airplanes, rockets, and blimps," said Stanley Farwell, construction superintendent. Then they turned to helicopters.

Kern pilots Charles E. Green, Jr., and Joe Chapman designed and built a spinning reel to lay the cable, slung it below the Bell 47G-2, and poised on the edge of the canyon for the descent. Green tells about the first flight.

"I climbed into the helicopter, hoping . . . that nothing fouled the cable. The descent was so steep that any braking or tension on the cable could have drawn it up into the main rotor blades. In which case, it goes without saying, I would have bought it—but good."

He took off and descended slowly, the helicopter on autorotation dropping like a parachute fall. The flight took only 2½ minutes. The rest of the operation was routine, except for a snarl in the heavier cable that was cleared by workmen carried in the helicopter to the trouble spot—an otherwise inaccessible ledge.

The Belgians were quick to recognize the helicopter as peculiarly suited to that small country's transportation needs. For a few years, Sabena, the government airline, flew scheduled passenger flights over a network that spanned half of Western Europe. Sabena started with a fleet of S-55s, the same machine (military H-19) that had made the first transatlantic helicopter flight in 1952. Experts say the venture failed only because the Belgians went into it before the proper machines came along.

A defective 200-foot smokestack in downtown Stockholm, Sweden, stood too close to other buildings for dynamiting, so a Bell 47 lowered a hook, grabbed a chunk of bricks, and pulled it down bit by bit, till the helicopter had nibbled it to the ground.

One of New York Airways' Boeing Vertol 107s that once flew from the airports to the Pan American Building roof in Manhattan. The machines went to the Pacific Northwest for use in logging. All U.S. helicopter lines and Sabena (Belgium) had to abandon scheduled passenger service.

On November 4, 1958, a worker's kerosene lamp exploded at the new but not quite completed Brussels airport, Sabena's headquarters, and set fire to the control tower. Perched 155 feet above the ground, towermen Marcel Courtoy and Guillaume Michaux sniffed smoke at about 9:45 P.M. They could have escaped then, but their duty was to clear all aircraft from the area. Just 11 minutes after their first alarm, it was too late for them to escape.

Smoke drove them from the glassed-in housing. They jumped to the roof eight feet below. Smoke and flames roared up an elevator shaft and poured from the windows. The towermen ran about looking for clear areas as the wind tore holes in the smoke. A crowd gathered below. Firemen tried to raise a ladder, but it was too short. The terminal also housed Sabena's helicopter hangar, and thinking more clearly than any of the others present, Courtoy shouted, "Send a helicopter!"

A phone call to the home of Armand Adam, Sabena's helicopter maintenance manager, brought him racing the mile and a half to the helicopter hangar. Adam described the rescue preparations:

"We pulled . . . the oldest S-58 we have from the hangar. We removed the two cabin doors, attached a heavy rope onto the cabin seats, and tied a shoulder harness to the rope. This is a safety harness used by our photographer during photo flights. The idea was to hover over the tower and pick up the men with the harness."

Another phone call brought Gerard Tremerie, Sabena's chief helicopter pilot. At the hangar, Tremerie called for a volunteer to work the rope and sling. Charles Gillet, a young inspector, climbed into the craft. So did the maintenance man Adam.

"It was amazing what Armand had done in the 10 minutes it took me to drive to the airport," Tremerie said. "Thirty seconds after I stepped from my car, we were in the air."

Over the fire, the turbulence was too great to hover, so Tremerie abandoned the sling idea. The two stranded men had fallen at one corner of the roof and were clearly in bad shape. The radio antennas and supporting wires that bristle over the roofs of all control towers threatened the helicopter's tail rotor. Tremerie managed to set down on the roof within a clear square only 45 feet on a side. He kept the blades turning to keep some of the craft's weight off the weakened roof.

"As we landed," Adam said, "the rotor downwash cleared a small area within the cloud of billowing smoke. The downwash also fed fresh air to the carburetor."

Although they were able to struggle to their feet, the towermen were confused and tried to claw their way into a closed emergency door on the helicopter's port side. Adam and Gillet leaped out to the smoking roof and lead the towermen to the open doors on the starboard side. Adam prowled about the roof to be sure nobody else was lying unconscious in the smoke. He remounted the helicopter, and within seconds Tremerie landed at the hangar. It was 10:35. Only 15 minutes had elapsed since Adam had been told there were men trapped on the tower.

The next day, Tremerie received a letter from Courtoy's eight-year-old daughter, Suzanne, which read:

"How happy I am, sir, because you have brought back my dad before he burned. Thank you very much. I send you my best kiss from me, and kisses from my younger sisters Colette and Monique, and my brother Marcel who cannot yet write."

Behind the Iron Curtain, helicopter development went on apace. In May 1959, Ralph P. Alex, president of the American Helicopter Society, visited Russia to study the Soviets' progress.

He reported that the tandem-rotor "Horse" (Yak-24) lifted and carried trucks of up to five tons and that future models would be designed to accommodate 40 passengers over short hauls. The smaller "Hound" (Mil-4) carried up to 20 passengers. Both craft had a range of 300 miles. The "Hen" (Kamov-15) flew a pilot, a passenger, and 110 pounds of luggage 155 miles at 100 miles per

hour. The "Hook" (Mil-6), a powerful machine, had reportedly lifted five tons to an astonishing 18,207 feet. Its passenger capacity for comfortable seating was 70 to 80; with a bit of crowding, the "Hook" would accommodate up to 120 persons.

All Russian craft were rigged for de-icing. Mr. Alex also reported seeing evidence that the Russians were arming helicopters with light and heavy machine guns, rockets, and cannon, placing emphasis on rocket systems. Although photographs of the Russian craft showed they lacked the graceful lines of American counterparts, their performance was evidence that the Soviets possessed formidable helicopter technology.

In March 1958, the Marines had launched a long-dreamed-of exercise in seaborne vertical assault. Lying to off Onslow Beach, North Carolina, the carriers U.S.S. *Tarawa, Forrestal,* and *Valley Forge* launched an assault wave of light helicopters carrying troops and light equipment, followed by the supply wave carrying the heavy stuff. The choppers dropped a beefed-up Marine regiment of 6,000 men with 100 vehicles and supplies 50 miles inland. A reinforced Marine regiment is a formidable fighting machine indeed, and only 60 helicopters flying 2,000 sorties were needed to leapfrog that mighty force clean over the vulnerable landing beaches and deep behind hypothetical enemy lines.

After that day's lesson, Marine assault tactics never turned back to massed amphibious landings on the beaches.

Impressed by the Marines' success with vertical envelopment, the U.S. Navy converted several aircraft carriers to assault helicopter carriers, then built two, the U.S.S. *Iwo Jima* and the *Okinawa,* from the keel up as helicopter carriers.

From one of the converted carriers, the U.S.S. *Thetis Bay,* choppers flew 898 missions to save lives during floods on Taiwan. Another carrier, the U.S.S. *Yorktown,* rushed to the relief of the British freighter *Shun Lee,* driven aground by Typhoon Mary on Pratas Reef 500 miles northwest of Manila, the Philippines. One sailor had been lost,

Five of these powerful single-seaters were built in England for a U.S. Marine Corps experimental program. They will climb to an astounding 13,000 feet. The last one was built in 1960.

The tanker *African Queen* ran aground off Ocean City, Maryland, in 1958. Seas were so rough the ship broke in two—the structure in the foreground is part of the forward half—and surface craft could not approach to attempt a rescue. The U.S. Coast Guard coordinated a helicopter rescue in a shuttle that lifted 45 crewmen to safety.

29 had fled the ship by lifeboat and were perilously installed on a Pratas island sandbar, and 24 others, including the captain, remained on the ship. The British frigate *Torquay* was standing by but could not approach the wreck because of high seas.

While still 50 miles off, the *Yorktown* launched seven helicopters. One lowered a flight surgeon to the island, and the others rushed to remove the 24 men from the ship, one at a time. One injured sailor had to be lashed to the sling. After finishing with the ship, the helicopters picked up the sailors shipwrecked on the island.

Across the Pacific, on May 21-22, 1960, then again from May 27 and into June, terrible earthquakes and tidal waves ravaged Chile, killing 5,700 persons, destroying tens of thousands of

On his way to demonstrate a Bell helicopter to law enforcement officers of the Minneapolis-St. Paul region, Ed Goshorn made a routine landing at police dispatch headquarters. Without even properly introducing himself, a trooper leaped aboard. "Let's go," he shouted. "Two trusties just escaped from the Minnesota State Farm." Immediately after takeoff, Goshorn spotted the pair in a grove. He ordered them out with hands up. Alerted by radio, police were waiting with handcuffs. Newsmen photographed the pair emerging from the woods with the helicopter shepherding overhead. The sheriff announced on the spot he was buying a Bell 47G-2.

In November 1959, Typhoon Vera ravaged Japan, causing floods in low-lying areas. The rescue craft evacuating these flood victims are U.S. Navy Sikorsky HSS helicopters.

homes, and lifting new islands from the sea while submerging others. Entire coastal villages disappeared.

Ready for just such a disaster was the new Bell HU-1A Iroquois, a superb turbine jet-powered helicopter. Although it has found dozens of other uses, the Iroquois was built as an ambulance. Designed for a two-man crew and six passengers, the tough little craft has carried 10 fully equipped soldiers on maneuvers.

Immediately after the first shocks on May 21-22, the U.S. Department of Defense ordered 10 Iroquois knocked down and loaded aboard C-124 cargo carriers of the Military Air Transport Service. The helicopters were accompanied by 40 pilots and crew members. Two medical detachments, organized and trained to work with helicopters, came from Fort Bragg, North Carolina, and Fort Meade, Maryland. A transport company from Fort Bragg tagged along.

During the night of May 26, while the quakes were gathering strength for a second blow, the cargo planes took off for Chile. By May 30, a field hospital was in operation on a football field next to a Chilean hospital destroyed in the quakes. The next day, the reassembled Iroquois were flying. With a 200-mile range and 14,000-foot

ceiling, the Iroquois prowled through a pall of smoke and cold rains, searching for survivors isolated in the mountains. They airlifted more than 200 of the injured and carried in medical corpsmen to vaccinate 600 others in three days alone as disease threatened to increase the earthquake's horror. In less than a week, the helicopters transported 8½ tons of medical supplies and food to stranded villages.

Early in the space program, the helicopter became the workhorse of both astronaut and capsule recovery. On January 31, 1960, a Marine helicopter picked up a Mercury capsule from the splashdown, 420 miles downrange from Cape Canaveral. The capsule had made a 155-mile-high loop into space. Television cameramen recorded the touching scene when the capsule was opened aboard the recovery ship and the passenger—a

The Washington State Game Department hit upon the idea of using helicopters to herd elk to winter feeding grounds at Oak Creek, thus drawing them away from the Yakima Valley orchards.

The Hiller 12E deserved its reputation for maneuverability as shown in this famous photograph taken in 1960. The three-seater machine competed with the Bell 47G for all-around versatility.

chimpanzee named Ham—blinked, searched the crowd for a familiar face, and held out his arms with a smile to his trainer. The trainer's eyes unashamedly filled with tears.

On May 4, 1961, a gigantic balloon called the *Stratolab* took off from the U.S.S. *Antietam* near the mouth of the Mississippi River to collect high-altitude data for future spaceflights. In the two-place gondola were Comdr. Malcolm D. Ross and Lt. Comdr. Victor A. Prather, a medical doctor. They soared to a record 113,740 feet and touched down in the Gulf of Mexico, 136 miles south of Mobile, Alabama.

Tragically, after having survived the balloon flight, Dr. Prather fell from the recovery helicopter's sling and died an hour later. All chopper pilots cursed the sling, already abandoned by the Coast Guard, but it remained standard equipment on most helicopters for at least another 10 years.

The day after Dr. Prather's death, May 5, 1961, astronaut Alan B. Shepard, Jr., rode the Mercury capsule Freedom 7 from Cape Canaveral to an altitude of 116 miles, America's first manned venture into space. Downrange, near the planned splashdown point, two Marine pilots, 1st Lts. Wayne E. Koons and George F. Cox, circled in a Sikorsky HUS-1 (civilian S-58) at 500 feet. They picked up Shepard's radio transmission when the capsule had descended to 85,000 feet. As the capsule passed 20,000 feet, the helicopter radio direction-finder began tracking the descent. The pilots sighted the capsule at 7,000 feet and were hovering 100 feet over the capsule while it was still bobbing from impact.

Cox slipped back to the hoist operator's position. Koons flew by the floating capsule at wave-top level. Cox coached him into position, reached over with a pole armed with a hook (nicknamed, naturally, the Shepard's crook), and slipped the hook through a nylon loop on top of the capsule.

"We have a good hookup," he told the pilot.

Koons lifted till the capsule swung clear of the water, an astonishing 3½ minutes after impact. Cox lowered the sling to Shepard, who was

In a virtuoso performance, the pilot of this Hiller 12E placed 40 poles up a mountainside in the Pacific Northwest in less than four hours and followed the act by laying two manila "sock lines" along the three-mile right-of-way in 12 minutes. Performed in 1961, this feat established the Hiller as the tool of choice when laying telephone lines in terrain so steep the ground crew has to stand with one leg on a stump to hold an even keel.

standing in the capsule's hatch. The astronaut rode to safety in the cabin of the recovery craft. The helicopter landed the capsule on the U.S.S. *Lake Champlain*, then landed itself a few feet away. Commander Shepard stepped out to as wild a demonstration of enthusiasm as the navy permits itself.

The recovery of Virgil I. Grissom on July 21, 1961, was a much closer thing. Grissom rode a capsule for a 118-mile spaceflight and splashed down 303 miles downrange. Recovery forces abandoned all routine procedures when the hatch accidentally blew off and seas swamped the capsule. Grissom was swimming, but his space suit was rapidly filling with water and dragging him down. Encumbered by the water-filled suit, Grissom could not throw the sling properly over his head and under his arms. In desperation, he slid into it backward and was hoisted aboard, narrowly missing a repetition of Dr. Prather's accident.

After John H. Glenn, Jr., made the first American manned orbital flight in the Mercury capsule *Friendship 7* on February 20, 1962, he came down in the Atlantic Ocean, east of the Bahamas. Warned by Grissom's near tragedy, Glenn kept the capsule closed till it was picked up by the destroyer U.S.S. *Noa*. After climbing out, he was lifted by a navy helicopter to the U.S.S. *Randolph* for a phone conversation with President John F. Kennedy.

The recovery after the second American manned orbital spaceflight on May 24, 1962, was again a near tragedy. Astronaut M. Scott Carpenter splashed down in the Atlantic Ocean, about 250 miles beyond the scheduled site. While millions of his countrymen worried, planes searched for two hours, till a navy Neptune found the capsule. An air force plane dropped a parachute team to buoy the capsule with a flotation collar.

A navy HSS-2, fortunately a very fast helicopter, arrived an hour later and carried Carpenter to the U.S.S. *Intrepid*, to the immense relief of the television audience, which had grown by the millions during the tense vigil.

After his orbital flight on October 3, 1962, Walter M. Schirra, Jr., came down in the Pacific Ocean, his capsule landing only four miles from the scheduled site. It was the first acceptably accurate splashdown in American space experience. A helicopter dropped swimmers to help him, but Schirra elected to stay in the capsule till it was lifted aboard the U.S.S. *Kearsarge*.

On August 4, 1961, fierce fires raged in the Douglas fir forests of Idaho and Montana. Twenty smoke jumpers, led by veteran Fred Wolfrum, parachuted into the forest near Higgins Ridge, Idaho. The fire fighters, most of them college youngsters on part-time duty, were making routine headway against the blaze when a fast-moving front with high winds swept through the forest. The fire leaped from the forest floor to the crown, and flames whipped through the treetops faster than a man can run.

Wolfrum rounded up his men and took refuge at the helistop clearing atop 7,000-foot-high Higgins Ridge.

"Normally, we would have hiked out of the danger area," Wolfrum said, "but by 4:30 I knew we were trapped." Wolfrum feared some of his boys would panic. "If anybody had tried to run out of that spot, it would have been too bad. In all likelihood, they would have stumbled and fallen, and that hot ash would have finished them."

The men had no radio and had to wait helplessly, hoping an aircraft would stumble across their trap. The flames made their helmets and canteens too hot to touch. Hot ashes covered the ground and the fire fighters had to hop about to keep the heat from blistering their feet. One man's pants caught fire. Another, who wore a short-sleeved shirt, suffered burns on the arms. The flames devoured oxygen, so the trapped men had to move about the helistop gasping, in search of fugitive currents of breathable air.

Late in the afternoon, somebody called for quiet; he thought he had heard a chopper. The men peered through the smoke.

To save work crews a 2½-hour trip up the steep canyon walls (left), the powerful Hiller 12E in 1963 carried men and equipment for power-line construction to a mountainside so steep it had to unload passengers by pushing the tips of its floats against the slope and hovering.

Despite the elevation, a Hiller 12E, the mighty midget, hovers in a 45-mile-per-hour wind near the top of a 10,000-foot mountain lifting a pole that weighs almost half as much as the machine itself. Between lifting jobs, the helicopter patrolled 204 miles of power line for the Pacific Power and Light Company, doing in eight hours what a ground crew would do in three weeks.

Braving the 60-mile-per-hour wind, Rodney Snider, with forest ranger William R. Magnuson as lookout, was searching for the lost party in a Bell 47G-3. About 5:30 P.M., he spotted the party and was appalled by their situation. He decided on instant action. Although the heat made the density altitude at 7,000 feet the equivalent of that at 12,500 feet—just about the helicopter's limit—Snider landed on the smoking, hot helistop and ferried out the men, landing the last fire fighter in safety at 8:00 P.M.

Interviewed about his heroic rescue, the 31-year-old Snider said of the helicopter, "A great ship. We just changed the oil."

The New Orleans Coast Guard air station was the first one to be all-helicopter equipped. Early in 1963, the Coast Guard gave the last of its old P5M seaplanes to the navy. Nobody mourned their passing, for they had been slow and heavy. The old HO4S helicopters that replaced them were only a slight improvement. Commander George Thometz (who had won the Distinguished Flying

On February 7, 1962, the S.S. *Chickasaw* carrying plywood, auto parts, toys, mirrors, burlap, and
95 cartons of baseball equipment from Japan to Canada went aground on Santa Rosa Island,
west of the California coast. A Hiller 12E belonging to Columbia Helicopters, Incorporated, of
Portland, Oregon, shuttled between the stricken vessel and various salvage craft carrying men
and equipment. Columbia Helicopters, among the most innovative of commercial operators, is
one of the pioneers in logging by rotary-wing craft.

Cross in the California floods of 1955) complained
that the craft "has the stability and buoyancy of a
brick." Thometz knew what he was talking about;
one had sunk under him two minutes after ditching in it.

Within weeks, three new HH-52A helicopters
arrived. They had amphibious hulls, an enormous

morale factor in an area divided between the Gulf
of Mexico and the Louisiana marshes, where it is
hard to tell at what point the land quits and the
water begins.

Piloted by Lt. Comdr. Glen Parsons, one of
the new helicopters soon demonstrated the value
of the floatable hull. The boat carrying a priest

Left: Environmental scientists fly to remote areas along a proposed pipeline route looking over the terrain to estimate the impact of construction work.

Jim Klotz was airlifting 800-pound sections of dredge pipe nearby when the self-unloader M.V. *Alaska Cedar* went aground in 1963. A rescue team rigged a breaches line, visible from the fore part of the pilot house, to the beach, but the helicopter provided speedier transfer of injured crewmen to a Coast Guard station.

and a little girl fishing on Lake Pontchartrain capsized and threw them into the water. The priest tied himself to the bow of the boat and held the little girl's head above water while he waited for rescue. Night fell, and the priest faced long hours of waiting for dawn in the chilly lake. He was not sure his strength would hold out or that the girl could survive the exposure.

Miraculously, Parsons found them after midnight and landed on the rough water. The priest tried to hand up the child, but he was too exhausted, and she fell from his hands. The crewman, James B. Reynolds, dived overboard and found the girl deep under the waves. He carried her to the surface and handed her up to the co-

pilot. Reynolds cut the priest loose but could not get a purchase for his feet in the open water in order to lift him aboard. The crewman dived underwater, wrapped his arms around the priest's

When the men of the California highway patrol removed 35,000 abandoned cars from the roads, they found several hundred auto carcasses near Palos Verdes which had been pushed over the cliffs and into the sea. Helicopters picked them out, leaving an impeccable beach for vacationers.

Air-sea rescue operations became easier when the Sea-series helicopters appeared. The two shown below are the Boeing Vertol Sea Knight (top) and the Kaman Seasprite. Their floating hulls make possible direct pickups from the water whenever weather permits. High seas, however, could force hoist pickup as in the scene (right) of a real rescue of a boating party clinging to their capsized craft.

legs, and pulled the CO_2 latch on his life jacket. The inflating jacket lifted him and the priest like an elevator, and the priest rolled aboard the chopper.

At Coast Guard headquarters, over a cup of hot coffee, the priest confessed that he had resigned himself to a "transfer to Headquarters."

By 1963 conservation agencies had discovered the helicopter's versatility. In New Mexico, a Bell 47G-3B helicopter sowed about a hundred thousand trout fry into wilderness lakes.

In Labrador, conservation workers lassoed caribou as they swam a stream, tranquilized them, wrapped them in canvas tarpaulins to protect them from the wind, slung them on wooden pallets under helicopters, and flew them out of the forest. Planes then flew six males and 18 females to Mount Katahdin in Maine. There helicopters released them in woods where they had been extinct since the nineteenth century.

In an effort to keep track of some 125,000 moose in the province, Ontario's Department of Lands and Forests has engaged helicopter pilots flying Bell 47-Gs to buzz moose and drive them into lakes. As the moose swim, the helicopter settles over them and straddles them with floats so that a department research scientist can pop a metal tag into one of their ears. The procedure, developed by chopper pilot Ben Kent and several biologists, takes about five minutes. Tags returned by hunters tell the department where the animals are being overhunted and where they need thinning because they are overbrowsing the range.

Growth of aquatic plants in Princeton University's Lake Carnegie had plagued rowing crews for years. Dredging had done little to clear the lake. A helicopter, piloted, as it happened, by Charles P. Logg, Jr., a gold medalist oarsman in the 1952 Olympics, treated the lake with a herbicide harmless to fish and cleared a course for the racing shells.

In the Pacific Northwest, the Weyerhaeuser Company had begun experimenting with helicopter forest seeding as early as 1950. Birds and mice ate half the seed drop, however, so Weyerhaeuser applied a repellent powder to the seeds. Experiments showed that helicopter reseeding worked best immediately after logging, during which the ground was churned loose by tractor cleats and dragging logs and the brush effectively removed. Seeding with fixed-wing craft had not been successful. Timbermen in Louisiana dis-

The Church of Altötting (bottom), known as the Lourdes of Germany, needed a new steeple after centuries of weathering. The U.S. Army Sikorskys lifted the 82-foot spire in three sections. The whole town of 10,000 turned out to supervise the job. Dr. Robert Bauer, administrator of the shrine, said: "As long as the renewed spire of the holy shrine stands—and we hope it stands for centuries—it will give notice of the kindness of American forces and American people." He might have added that it will give notice of the handiness of helicopters. Right: A cross being placed atop another German church.

Cattlemen quickly took to helicopters for spotting strays and riding fence, and even used them for herding during roundups.

covered that a helicopter fitted with hoppers carrying loblolly pine seeds could sow an eight-acre area per minute, as opposed to an airplane's record of 30 minutes for the same patch.

Helicopters played quite a different wildlife role in the Gulf of St. Lawrence, where a Bell 47D-1 flew from the sealer *North Star VI* to lead a sealing convoy through heavy ice to the killing grounds. The chopper spotted calving herds, flew the killers in and the pelts out. It also carried out injured crewmen.

Rotary-wing pilots have invariably coaxed better performances from their machines than the manufacturers claimed for the craft. Rescue fliers in particular routinely exceeded the speed, altitude, and load-capacity limits as the occasion demanded.

During the floods in Morocco in January 1963, a Bell UH-1B, an improved version of the Iroquois, set a staggering lift record. Designed to carry a two-man crew and seven passengers, the Iroquois regularly carried 22 or more on a single lift. Hard as the story is to believe, it is well documented. Harold K. Milks, chief of the Associated Press bureau in Madrid, witnessed one such flight and reported it.

"U.S. Army Capt. Donald G. Murphey appealed for 'just one more flight' when the rescue operations director ordered a halt to the helicopter operations when darkness fell.

" 'I can't stop now,' Captain Murphey insisted as he unloaded a helicopter filled with refugees. 'When we left that village, there were still 11 kids on the rooftop, and I've got to bring them in.'

One of the most aggressive and imaginative commercial helicopter operators is Ostermans of Sweden. Here an Ostermans machine is lifting into place a directional antenna atop a 240-foot television broadcasting tower in Stockholm.

"Colonel Warren D. Johnson, Sidi Slimane base commander directing the air force-army-navy joint rescue efforts, gave his permission for another flight, after arranging emergency lights to mark Murphey's landing area.

"Forty minutes later, Murphey and his copilot, Capt. Ernest D. French, came chugging back through the darkness, their single-engined Bell UH-1B helicopter barely skimming above the water.

"They landed, and out climbed the 11 Moroccan kids, plus 11 Moroccan adults. Someway, and Murphey said he wasn't sure just how, 22 passengers and a crew of three had flown back in a helicopter designed for a maximum of seven passengers."

The army's own *Aviation Digest* for April 1963 reported that an army Iroquois No. 61-699 carried 32 refugees plus an interpreter, crew chief, and pilot. The crewman and interpreter had to stand on the helicopter's skids. At the Sidi Slimane Air Force Base, astonished officers were logging in 20 to 25 refugees on every rescue trip of the Iroquois. In five days, the Iroquois had evacuated 1,400 and had made countless food drops.

On February 4, 1963, three other improved Iroquois helicopters, performing mapping duty with Operation Deep Freeze, flew 165 miles from 9,000-foot Mount Weaver to the American camp at the South Pole, thus becoming the first helicopters to set down at the bottom of the world.

A few months later, in cold about as brutal as the South Pole's, an American mountaineering team made a double assault on Mount Everest, in

Long before the movie Jaws, *a Kaman helicopter flew a Connecticut Board of Fisheries biologist named Richard Hames along the state's beaches in a pre-Labor Day search for sharks. He reported none.*

By carrying surveying crews to 75 mountain peaks where they set up electronic devices for measurements accurate to 12 inches within 20 miles, two Bell Iroquois made possible mapping of 85,000 square miles of Antarctica in 57 operating days.

Helicopters are low-level craft and perform poorly at high altitudes where the air is too thin for the rotary blades to take a good bite. Nevertheless, when a call to rescue stranded climbers injured in a fall on Mount McKinley, highest peak in North America, reached him at Anchorage, Alaska, Link Luckett stripped his Hiller 12E of all excess weight, including the battery, and flew to 17,230 feet for the pickups. Not only was it the highest rescue on record to that date, but it was the highest takeoff and landing of any kind of aircraft in history. Furthermore, he had to make three landings on two days, May 20–21, 1960.

the Himalayas. William Unsoeld of Corvallis, Oregon, and Dr. Thomas F. Hornbein of San Diego, California, climbed the hitherto unscaled west ridge to the 29,028-foot summit. Barry C. Bishop, a National Geographic Society staffer from Washington, D.C., and Luther G. Jerstad of Eugene, Oregon, reached the summit by the traditional South Col route. A savage blizzard blew away blankets and tent, so the four had to spend the night unsheltered at 28,000 feet. Unsoeld and Bishop suffered severe frostbite of the feet. The American embassy sent the only helicopter in Nepal, a Bell 47G-3 of Ostermans Overseas Aviation, under charter to the American aid mission. On May 27, the chopper picked up the two frostbitten climbers at a 12,000-foot-high Nepalese village and in less than two hours flew them to the United Mission hospital at Katmandu, Nepal's capital. Because of quick treatment, they lost only the tips of their toes. The other members of the party took two weeks to walk back.

Deep in the jungles of trans-Andean Peru, there unfolded a drama worthy of the most lurid B-grade adventure movie. In March 1964, a survey party of 42 men, cutting a 90-mile right-of-way for a proposed highway, ran into an ambush by Mayoruna Indians—a tribe hostile to outsiders and very primitive, but not so primitive that they were not armed with shotguns and muzzle-loading muskets. (South American arms manufacturers still did a brisk trade in crude muzzle-loaders because the weapons could fire rocks when the Indians ran out of bullets.) Two of the surveyors were severely wounded and a third killed.

The men, led by Gumercindo do Flores, the mayor of Requena, had expected trouble before the ambush. They had holed up in an abandoned hut, torn up another one to put up a wooden barricade, added a mud parapet, and waited for an attack.

By radio the surveyors reported to the military base at Requena that they could see no Indians but had heard bird cries all night—cries of day birds, indicating they were signals of besieg-

ing warriors. Mayor do Flores described the ambush of the 11-man patrol he had sent out and asked Requena for help.

The beleaguered men were running out of the food they had looted from a nearby Indian village, and a drop by planes took care of this problem. But now they were low on water. Fifteen of them volunteered to make a dash for water, carrying an aluminum cooking pot to a stream at the edge of the jungle.

While they were filling the pot, a voice from the jungle boomed the war cry "Cumpahoo," and shotguns crashed through the foliage, bringing down three of the water detail. The rest fired blindly into the jungle, and several of their comrades in the fortress-hut came running to the rescue.

Most of the jabbering in the jungle was in an unknown Indian language. Then a voice rang out in purest Spanish, "Cowards! Fags! Come after us and fight!" The quality of the Spanish was far better than could be expected of a mission-educated Indian much less of a primitive Mayoruna, so the war party was almost certainly led by a renegade white.

The rescue party carried their three wounded back to the hut. One of them had taken nine buckshot pellets in the leg, side, and arm at point-blank range; another had taken a frightful 32 pellets in the back and one in the neck, a finger's breadth from the jugular. The third man, a relative of the man killed in the first ambush, died within minutes from his wounds.

The radio operator, Sergeant Castillo, reported this second attack to the air base at Iquitos, on the upper reaches of the Amazon, and again asked for help. Two fighter-bombers came in to work over the jungle with antipersonnel bombs and machine-gun fire. The defenders cursed the bombers for concentrating on one small spot in the jungle instead of raking the area in a ring around the fort. Apparently, from their lofty perch, the pilots could see a concentration of Indians the besieged could not, for shortly after the planes

Bantus exorcise a Bell 47J-2 in Johannesburg, South Africa.

left, a great cloud of buzzards spiraled into the strike zone, indicating a major kill.

To complicate the defenders' plight, a jungle fever struck the fort, keeping the two medical corpsmen running between the ill and the wounded. Mayor do Flores radioed Requena, recommending that helicopters be sent in to lift them out. The men cleared a landing area and set fire to the nearby hut to prevent its use as cover in another attack.

The next day, when Do Flores tried to contact Requena again, the radio burned out, cutting their last link with the outside.

Already the siege had become front-page news around the world. Correspondents from major South American papers were gathering at the forward base in Peru to send out hourly bulletins.

Answering an appeal from the Peruvian Air Ministry, Maj. Burton MacKenzie, chief of the U.S. Air Force mission, called Panama. There, U.S. Marines dismantled two Kaman helicopters and loaded them aboard two giant C-130 Hercules cargo planes. At 4:00 A.M. on March 20, 1964, the Hercules transports took off on the 1,500-mile flight, just 14 hours after Major MacKenzie first asked for help. They carried Maj. Ray Uribe of the U.S. Air Force because he was fluent in Spanish. In three hours, the planes circled over Iquitos, the airfield nearest the Indian fight.

When the pilots broke through low-scudding rain clouds, they saw hundreds of workers repairing rain damage to the frighteningly short runway. They made one turn to check over the field and then came in like carrier fighters, chopping power at the last second and dropping like rocks to the runway, then reversing their props with a deafening roar. They stopped just short of the ditch at the runway's end. The Marines immediately began reassembling the Kamans.

In the jungle, the besieged had a new radio that had been dropped by plane, but their reports were discouraging. Fever was spreading. Mayor do Flores said he no longer had enough men in shape to fight off a charge.

Marine mechanics finished reassembling the helicopters at midnight. But the craft could not take off, for it was too far from Iquitos to the grass and mud fortress under siege. Riverboatmen carried 55-gallon drums of fuel to Requena, the intermediate base, and to Curinga, only 20 miles from the battle site, but the operation took several days. Then steady equatorial rains made it impossible to fly out, so the helicopters remained grounded.

At the first appearance of a patch of blue in the sky, the helicopters took off for the clearing after refueling stops at Requena and Curinga. The choppers were manned by Capt. Royal Moore and WO Robert Norton as pilots, Lt. José Pinedo of the Peruvian Air Force (the pilot who had first found the clearing) as guide, and Maj. Fernando Melzi as Peruvian coordinator.

Because of the peculiar arrangement of rotors on a Kaman, it can be approached only by a narrow path from the rear.

"Stay 15 yards away from the helicopters," the radio warned the defenders. "Wait until you see a man leave the helicopters. He will then lead you. . . . Do *not* approach the helicopters until you are led by personnel aboard. To do so will mean death."

The defenders loaded stretchers with the sick and wounded and crouched in a ring, their guns trained on the jungle. Knowing that an educated white man was with the Indians, Mayor do Flores feared that the renegade would know the sound of helicopters and might well lead a last-minute charge to thwart the rescue.

"Get back to back," Do Flores said, "and if necessary, fight until everybody is dead."

The first chopper banked about the clearing and sank to the ground, throwing up a dense cloud of dust from the downwash. Major Melzi jumped out, armed with a welcome submachine gun tucked under one arm. With the other arm, he showed the safe route under the whirling blades. The first helicopter took off with two litter cases and a walking wounded. Major Melzi remained behind, training his submachine gun on the jungle.

Circling overhead was a Peruvian C-47 transport, carrying Gen. Nestor Mendoza, the regional army commander, and a platoon of newsmen from all over South America. A U.S. Army sergeant even made movies of the rescue.

Between helicopter trips, Major Melzi crouched with the remaining survivors behind the hastily constructed mud barricade. His submachine gun brought them a great upsurge of confidence during the shuttle flights. It was late in the afternoon when Major Melzi mounted a helicopter, the last man to leave the clearing. The rescue was over, and the jungle reverted to the Indians and their mysterious renegade.

At Eglin Air Force Base, in Florida, a 75-foot ship went aground off the Florida beach. The pilot of a rescue helicopter noticed that during a scouting pass, his downwash had blown the bow free. The pilot came about, blew the ship out to sea, dropped a hawser to the skipper, and passed the other end to a crash boat for a tow to safety.

On August 7, 1964, just before sunset, Dick Irvin of San Jose, California, came running to the Skagit District ranger station in the North Cascade Mountains of Washington. Two of his fellow mountain climbers had taken a bad fall, he said, and urgently needed rescue.

One of the injured, Dave French of Berkeley, California, later recounted the accident.

"I was descending a 50-degree slope and had gone about five steps when a stone broke loose and I started to fall. I immediately went into a self-arrest position. I estimate that I slid about 50 feet.

"During the fall, I felt no tension until there was a sharp jerk. At about 50 feet, the rope went taut and then slack again. I looked up and saw that Fran [Mrs. David Stevenson] was falling down the slope toward me. She hit me and went over the top of me. We both continued to slide, and I was able to slow myself a little before hitting the rocks. I saw Fran go into the rocks and tumble through them, coming to rest 20 feet below me."

The injured woman's husband, Dr. Stevenson, hurried down the slope to her side. She had apparently suffered a dangerous neck injury. Her hard hat was cracked and deeply scoured where her head had hit the rocks. French had painful back injuries but was able to move about.

Three other climbers in the party descended to their base camp and told Irvin about the accident. He raced on foot 23 miles to the ranger station at Marblemount. A huge rescue effort got under way. Sheriff's office rescue units in three counties and the search and rescue unit of the naval air station at Whidbey Island began moving. Five Sierra Club climbers, who happened to be in the neighborhood, organized a team to carry sleeping bags, tarpaulins, air mattresses, warm clothing, food, water, and camp stoves to the accident site.

The navy launched a helicopter with Lt. John R. Greenway as pilot. The Kaman UH2B could not penetrate the dense cloud cover and gave up

till next morning. But fog continued to baffle the air searchers, so ground parties pressed forward. French had recovered enough to walk out, but Mrs. Stevenson was still at the accident site with her husband and Dick Brown of the Sierra Club relief party.

By noon the next day, E. G. Englebright, leading an advance rescue party, reached the scene. Shortly afterward other rescuers arrived and helped place Mrs. Stevenson on a Stokes litter. They belayed the stretcher 150 feet down the steep slope to a ledge a helicopter could approach without swiping its rotor blades against the mountainside. They rigged lines to the four corners of the stretcher. With ice axes, they lifted the stretcher at the center lash-up to be sure weight was evenly distributed, so the Stokes would not roll or tip during the dangerous pickup.

About 1:40 P.M., the overcast thinned somewhat, and Greenway circled about, trying to locate the ledge through the clouds. The ground rescue party set off orange flares, marking a glide path to the ledge.

Lieutenant Greenway described his next move.

"Shortly thereafter the clouds lifted enough for us to see the upper party. They were perched on a small ledge cropping out from a nearby sheer cliff.

"Upon checking the area, it was decided that it was impossible to land or hover at that position ... [to lighten weight] we let out the ranger on a rock drift at 7,000 feet, and we dumped about a thousand pounds of fuel from the aft tank and made a pass. The first pass was unsuccessful, as the helo sagged off nearly into the rocks.... The next attempt was from 60 feet above the rock point with the cable extended."

Englebright reported the ground action.

"We knew that the helicopter could not hover at that elevation, and we realized that we had to snap the stretcher into the hook while the helo was moving. This would require split-second timing. The stretcher ropes were being held in position by six of us, and Dr. Stevenson stood at the head of the stretcher, explaining to his wife what was going to happen."

On the next pass, Greenway's crewman, G. M. Weiser, dropped a cable and hook that bounced across the rocks toward the litter.

Rescuers snapped the hook through the litter sling, and the helicopter soared off, the stretcher dangling 35 feet below the craft and 1,000 feet above the glacier. Weiser winched up the cable and pulled the stretcher aboard.

"Got her!" shouted Lieutenant Greenway to the base camp's radio operator. "Sure scared hell out of me!"

5

The First Helicopter War

Even before the French signed the treaty with the Democratic Republic of Vietnam at Geneva on July 21, 1954, ending their embroilment in Indochina, the United States Military Assistance Advisory Group was on the scene. The group began actively advising the South Vietnamese Army on February 12, 1955. On May 5, 1961, President Kennedy announced that he was considering deploying U.S. armed forces in South Vietnam. Ten days later Marine Helicopter Squadron 162 moved in a battalion landing team.

On December 22, 1961, as a "training exercise," two army helicopter companies landed South Vietnamese troops on both sides of a mud-filled canal running through pineapple fields. The Viet Cong began shooting, and American forces had their baptism of fire in a new Asian war. How surprised American headquarters officers were at the enemy resistance during the training exercise is hard to say.

Less than two weeks later, on January 2, 1962, American fighting men got a bitter taste of what was to come. Two army helicopter companies flying unarmed machines moved 1,036 South Vietnamese regulars into a hole in the jungle near Ap Bac, about 50 miles from Saigon, in the Mekong Delta. Although the Vietnamese Army regulars outnumbered the Viet Cong guerrillas 10 to one, the soldiers refused to fight. Their shrinking from battle caused three American deaths and the loss of five helicopters.

The fiasco caused the U.S. Army to mount machine guns on their helicopters, and President Kennedy announced, without mentioning the Ap Bac action, that advisers in the future would shoot back.

To counter the advantage guerrillas have in jungle country, Americans and South Vietnamese dreamed up a tactic of hit-and-run strikes by helicopter. The first strike, supported by the tough Iroquois—the Bell UH-1A (former HU-1A), but better known as the Huey—caught the Viet Cong by surprise and dealt them a devastating blow. But the Viet Cong learned fast, and the second attempt was not nearly so much fun—for the attackers.

This time the landing force found the enemy camp deserted. Waiting till the helicopters had picked up two-thirds of the raiding force, the Viet Cong struck from the jungle at the outnumbered one-third left on the ground. The strike's planners had not provided a large enough landing zone; the Viet Cong pasted the postage-stamp-size clearing in the jungle with every weapon they owned.

Despite the intense fire, the troop-transport helicopters kept boring in to pick up their charges. Overhead, Capt. Ray Vining and Capt. Joseph Josh, flying the rescue and evacuation mission for the strike, watched the last aircraft taking off. It had reached about 100 feet when Captain Josh reported that a ball of orange flame from some

Arming of helicopters as gunships was a matter of improvising and experimenting in the early days of the Vietnam conflict, but eventually a kind of standard was developed as shown here. This Huey (UH-1B) of the 1st Cavalry Division mounted door machine guns and pods for firing folding-fin rockets.

kind of enemy weapon had hit the fleeing helicopter. Piloted by Maj. James Gray, the stricken chopper autorotated to a dangerously open clearing. Although the rescue craft landed only 50 feet from the downed helicopter, it was hidden under the loom of the very ridge that supported the Viet Cong anti-aircraft guns.

Of the eight South Vietnamese soldiers in the downed craft, three were dead. All three Americans were wounded. The crew chief, Bill Watkins, was severely hurt but kept his head. He stamped out the fire and forced the others to run to the rescue helicopter.

"They were all in shock," Captain Josh reported.

Captain Vining took off and came under fire, once he left the protection of the ridge's overhang, but escaped.

At that time, American forces in Vietnam numbered scarcely 8,000. The buildup continued steadily.

Early in 1965, the South Vietnamese political situation was in such turmoil that many Americans were ready to get out in despair. Then on February 7, 1965, the Viet Cong attacked a military adviser's compound at Pleiku, killing nine, wounding 76, and destroying many helicopters. In retaliation, the U.S.S. *Coral Sea, Hancock,* and *Ranger* launched fighter-bomber strikes at the North Vietnamese barracks near Dong Hoi.

Three nights later, the Viet Cong struck again, this time at the U.S. Army helicopter base near Qui Nhon, killing 23 Americans and wounding 21. This time U.S. carriers retaliated by launching 100 planes to strike the North Vietnamese barracks at Chanh Hoa. Lieutenant Commander R. H. Schumaker, flying an F8D, was shot down and captured, beginning the sad procession of American airmen into prison compounds.

On March 2, 1965, began the air operation against North Vietnam called Rolling Thunder. Major Ronald L. Ingraham and Capt. Joe Phelan,

Right, top: During the history-making first transit of the Northwest Passage by a commercial vessel, the S.S. *Manhattan,* watch officers on the icebreaker-tanker regularly launched a helicopter patrol to spot leads through the ice. Right, bottom: A party from the S.S. *Manhattan,* looking for a little rest and recreation on Greenland's icy shore, was brought to bay by a hostile dog pack from a nearby Indian village. A chopper lifted the men out before they lost any fabric from the seats of their pants.

The ubiquitous Huey was to the airmobile troops of the Vietnam conflict what the jeep was to the foot soldier of World War II. All the UH-1 series of helicopters were called Hueys in Vietnam. Those shown here are Bell Iroquois UH-1Ds.

Left: United States Coast Guard helicopters launched from icebreakers scouted the harsh world of the Northwest Passage for the S.S. *Manhattan.*

The Sikorsky HH-3E, the U.S. Air Force version of the S-61, became affectionately known as the Jolly Green Giant. Equipped with jungle penetrator and hoist, it figured in hundreds of rescues. Because of its watertight hull, it could land on the sea to pick up downed pilots.

flying Kaman Huskies, had hardly arrived at a forward base near the Demilitarized Zone when they were called out to rescue the pilot of an F-100 who had ditched at sea near Dong Hoi, 40 miles behind the enemy lines. Immediately after takeoff, they received a report of another F-100 down near a supply depot at Xom Bong, North Vietnam. The two pilots flew offshore to avoid detection. Phelan spotted a red flare eight miles

at sea and picked up a South Vietnamese pilot. Joined by navy Skyraiders, the Kamans headed inland 15 miles at treetop level. At the crash site, Phelan lowered para-rescueman Jon Young, who found a blood-stained helmet but no pilot. Ground fire hit the helicopter, so Phelan picked up his crewman and retired while the Skyraiders pounded the area. Although they gave up on the first flier, who had clearly been carried off, the helicopter

Dean F. Johnson of the First Marine Medical Battalion shouts to the ready room the condition of a wounded Marine just brought in by helicopter.

enemy presence, 1st Lt. Warren M. Petersen, Jr., decided the zone was quiet. Seconds after he settled down, the windshield disintegrated, and a bullet bored through his hard hat, cutting the wires to his earphones and passing out through the top of the hat. Other bullets cut the helicopter's hydraulic lines. The gushing fluid meant the craft had only minutes of flying time left.

Crewmen fired machine guns out the doors on both sides, and the chopper copilot pumped bullets from an automatic rifle. A crewman jumped out and pulled the wounded Marine aboard. The helicopter left but did not run out of fuel till it was within 100 yards of a medical company. Corpsmen rushed to the downed helicopter and carried the wounded Marine to an emergency operating room. The chopper had 13 holes in its carcass.

The first air ambulance unit in South Vietnam used the radio call "Dustoff." All subsequent helicopter ambulance units used the same call. By 1965 more than 90 percent of American wounded left the combat zone by a Dustoff helicopter. Any casualty was within a 25-minute flight of surgical help.

Stories of almost superhuman valor in the medical evacuation work are so commonplace they become monotonous.

Typical was the night patrol of Capt. Arthur A. Dittmeier of the Marines on June 12, 1965. He and three other chopper pilots had stumbled into a firefight between a platoon of Viet Cong and a squad of Marines.

"There were four birds," the captain reported. "We couldn't see anything on the ground except the tracers between the two sides. Two of our birds turned on their landing lights."

With astonishing insouciance, the helicopters took turns lowering themselves into the field of fire, their landing lights offering the choicest target within 50 miles. They lifted out not only the wounded but also the entire embattled squad.

The Marines were capable of almost the same kind of effort to save a helicopter. On July 6, 1965, a UH-1 lost engine power returning from an escort

pilots stumbled across another American three miles farther inland, busily burning his papers. Ingraham picked him up. At the base, Phelan found his craft had been holed in one blade.

The behind-the-lines rescue was a big deal in 1965. It was only one of hundreds to follow.

The South Vietnamese were suffering losses of one infantry battalion a week. President Lyndon B. Johnson authorized U.S. ground forces to give the South Vietnamese combat support, and he sent in another 21,000 troops, boosting the number of Americans in Vietnam to 74,500. Within weeks helicopters were lifting American soldiers on search-and-destroy missions. The United States was in the war up to its neck—or beyond. Rescue missions multiplied.

Flying low over a wounded Marine to test

Salvage helicopters paid for themselves several times over by bringing in hundreds of planes and helicopters downed in jungle and rice paddy.

mission. It autorotated to a river island 10 miles southeast of Da Nang. A companion Huey notified Da Nang base, then shot up the riverbanks to keep the Viet Cong busy till help arrived.

A helicopter brought in a repair team. The Viet Cong had begun sniping from the riverbank, only 100 yards away, but Marine Skyhawk jets arrived and raked both riverbanks with 20-mm. explosive cannon shells. Troop-carrying helicopters brought in a rifle company that checked out the island for enemy troops and set up a defensive perimeter. (As lagniappe to the main operation, the Marines seized a Viet Cong cache of 3,500 pounds of rice and corn.)

A Chinook unloads from the rear at a mountain outpost on a slope so steep that it cannot set down its wheels.

Other helicopters brought lunch at noon. Then 11 mechanics arrived to dismantle the Huey, and departing craft carried out the pieces. An ordnance man disarmed the rockets left in the pods and returned them to the base. In late afternoon, a helicopter picked up the confiscated grain and carried it to Da Nang for distribution to needy families. Near sunset a cargo helicopter hovered over the stripped hull while ground crews engaged cargo hooks, then the big chopper picked it off the island and carried it home.

The riflemen had been sporadically fighting off Viet Cong attacks all day, but they enjoyed a peaceful pickup and airlift home.

Another salvage operation began on July 2, 1965, when a helicopter was forced down into a rice paddy. The escort bird followed it down and unloaded South Vietnamese Special Forces troops to form a defense perimeter around the disabled helicopter. The escort carried the downed crew to safety and returned. The Viet Cong fought all day, but helicopters lifted out the crippled craft. During the operation, Cpl. Richard G. Howard, firing a door machine gun at the enemy, was wounded. But in the heat of battle, he felt no pain and was so busy firing he "didn't have time to stop to see how bad it was." He was the first casualty of his Marine Medium Helicopter Squadron in its first two weeks of combat.

Northwest of Da Nang, a 2,700-foot peak dominates the northern approaches to the base area. Its only drawback is that the habitable space at the top is about the size of two suburban living rooms. From that minuscule platform, the mountainsides fall away in steep cliffs. So tempting as an observation post was that inhospitable

Soldiers offloaded from a Chinook form a defense perimeter preparatory to setting up a reconnaissance and fire-support strongpoint. The outpost will be supplied by helicopter.

peak, however, that the Marines flew in telescopes on tripods, radios, rations, sandbagging tools, and enough Marines to defend the outpost against any Viet Cong willing to climb the steep slopes. The helicopters carrying them to what was named Wheeler's Landing (for Col. E. B. Wheeler, commanding the Third Marine Regiment) could put down only the two front wheels and had to hover while crews unloaded relief artillery spotters, rations, drinking water, and the mail. Once a week, crews rotated the duty of spotting gunfire for offshore destroyers and warning the air base of Viet Cong buildups. The most dangerous moments of the duty on the peak were the loadings and unloadings of helicopters sticking out over open space. One misstep and . . . .

Late in July 1965, a combined search-and-destroy mission based in Da Nang exercised all

hands in the new kind of coordinated warfare that had evolved with the helicopter's arrival on the battlefield.

At dawn one helicopter squadron lifted a company of the Fourth Marine Regiment while another squadron picked up South Vietnamese regulars. A Marine infantry company moved up the coast in U.S. Navy landing craft.

The target was a triangular peninsula bordered by the South China Sea and the Truong Giang River.

The seaborne Marines landed on the beach and swept clear a landing zone for the airborne Marines. Artillery pounded the distant South Vietnamese landing zone, then ceased firing to allow the Vietnamese assault company to unload from helicopters, amid smoking shell holes and the stench of burnt explosive. Overhead, Hueys pasted

Marine helicopters lift leathernecks into Vietnam battle zones for search-and-destroy missions. The Marines used vertical envelopment in combat for the first time in Korea.

A Marine UH-1E supports a search-and-destroy mission near Marble Mountain in Vietnam by firing rockets into the jungle.

Viet Cong positions and dropped red smoke flares to mark them for ground forces. South Vietnamese riding armored personnel carriers closed off the neck of the peninsula to prevent the enemy's escape. Even the South Vietnamese Junk Fleet-15 landed troops from its picturesque craft.

The combined forces suffered no losses; they killed 25 Viet Cong and captured more than 40.

A few weeks later, word arrived at Da Nang that 50 Viet Cong were shacking up every night in two villages 10 miles away and slipping away during daylight hours. Major Marc A. Moore suggested a night helicopter assault to trap the enemy force inside the villages. Because of the dangers of collision and loss of contact and coordination, helicopters had never been used in night landings. Every day was bringing new discoveries in the evolving helicopter war, however, so the Marines improvised an attack to be called Operation Midnight.

On Friday, the 13th of August, Lt. Col. Lloyd Childers, skipper of Marine Medium Helicopter Squadron 361, briefed the flight crews. "You have the dubious distinction of being the first men to fly a nighttime combat helicopter strike."

Just before midnight came the signal "Air-

So thoroughly committed to vertical envelopment are today's armed forces that even when they land on a beach they travel by helicopter and not by boat. These troops of the 101st Airborne Division are coming ashore in Vietnam in UH-1Ds.

borne." In staggered columns of twos, 22 helicopters lifted off. Marine artillery dropped shells around the landing zones to mask the sound of approaching helicopter engines. Artillery fire stopped four minutes before touchdown. Four armed helicopters patrolled overhead, hoping to draw fire from any Viet Cong whose sleep had been disturbed so they could pinpoint the VC's resistance. But the enemy had nerves of steel and slept through the cannonading.

The first wave of troop-carriers settled down and only a minute from landing called for parachute flares. An air force transport overhead dropped a pattern that lit at 3,000 feet and illuminated the valley like a ghastly science fiction sun. Every helicopter hit the designated landing zone with precision.

During the three-day infantry sweep that followed, Marines killed two VC and captured a rocket launcher and rockets plus many grenades. They rounded up 30 prisoners.

The first night helicopter assault force suffered no casualties or damage to equipment. And as a result, the helicopter's role in combat expanded once again.

Early in the Vietnam conflict, tacticians had worried that helicopters flew too low and too slow for combat use. Their evolution as combat weapons strikingly paralleled the World War I change of the airplane from an observation platform to a formidable killer. The first helicopters carried at most a pair of grease guns—light submachine guns of limited range and striking power. As the war ground along, helicopters acquired various combinations of weapons, some of them very fearsome indeed. A typical troop escort had a mount for two 7.62-mm. M60C flexibly mounted machine guns on each side of the aircraft. The pilot aimed and fired the four guns with a reflex-sight and pistol-grip control. Rocket pods carried 14 folding-fin 2.75-inch rockets. The crew chief and gunner manned M-60 machine guns, mounted in the doors

As the role of the helicopter in combat operations mounted in Vietnam, commanders sent massed fleets into battle, the gunships battering the terrain to clear the way for troop transport landings. Evolution of the helicopter from a toothless Florence Nightingale into a tiger was the foremost military development of the Vietnam conflict.

for firing to the side and rear. Of the 6,800 rounds of ammunition aboard, every fifth was a tracer. The gunships also carried red, green, and yellow smoke grenades to mark strike zones for jet fighter-bombers. Other gunships fired grenade launchers capable of socking an area with 200 grenades per minute at a range of 1,000 yards. Ordnance experts continually tinkered with helicopter armament, seeking the best combination of weapons.

The fearsome firepower developed by the helicopter gunship is here displayed. Spread out are 2.75-inch rockets, grenade launchers, 30-caliber machine guns, and TOW missiles. Even in their early stage of development, TOW missiles, shown here standing on their fins, are formidable antitank weapons and have already revolutionized antitank tactics.

In the Mekong Delta of Vietnam, the U.S. Navy discovered an affinity between helicopter gunships (a trick frankly learned from the army) and their river-patrol gunboats. When the patrol boats ran into an ambush from shore, the helicopter squadron beat up the banks with rockets and machine-gun fire. Here two Huey gunships paste a Viet Cong nest in the delta 50 miles southwest of Saigon.

By August 18, 1965, when the Marines mounted a major push called Operation Starlight, their supporting helicopters had evolved from vulnerable pigeons to ferocious hawks.

The helicopter of 1st Lt. Norman E. Ehlert, one of two on patrol 12 miles south of Chu Lai, began to draw small-arms fire from the ground. There was the time when the helicopter would have fled. Times had changed.

"I thought there might be a target," Lieutenant Ehlert reported, "so I turned the bird and headed

Helicopters carrying South Vietnamese troops became flying barnyards. Because they had no refrigeration or C rations, Vietnamese troops carried pigs, ducks, chickens, and occasionally a litter of puppies. They also carried melons, tomatoes, squash, cabbage, pots and pans, and even firewood.

Helicopter crews soon lost their ability to be surprised by the cargoes they carried. When they transported South Vietnamese troops, the choppers also carried chickens, pigs, goats, cattle, wives, children, and litters of puppies.

When Capt. James F. Pleva's Sea Knight caught fire after being hit by the enemy, he doused the flames by landing in a mountain stream. The craft was recovered.

back over the zone. Then everything opened up at once. My chopper was hit in the rotor blades first, and a few seconds later, they got us in the tail section. It didn't do the VC any good though. I had them spotted on a long ridgeline . . . and we were still flying."

Lieutenant Ehlert dived on the ridge and raked it with a ripple of 36 rockets. The door gunners fired short bursts into the flanks of the enemy line.

He landed to replace the riddled blade and returned to battle. During the day of working over enemy positions, his craft suffered nine more hits but kept on flying.

Lieutenant Ehlert spotted a cluster of enemy mortars, just as a flight of Phantom jets came

over. He could not pass up the chance, so he asked the jet fighter-bombers to stand by while he marked the mortars with a smoke bomb. His craft shuddered again as it was hit for the tenth time.

"The left gunner has been hit bad," yelled Sgt. Robert L. Brazke over the intercom. He gave what first aid he could to his wounded comrade and returned to his machine gun for the flight back to the base.

In the same sky, Lieutenant Ehlert's patrol mate, Maj. Donald J. Reilly, was smoke bombing targets for jet fighters when Lance Cpl. Marc S. Czomba, who had just thrown a smoke grenade and was looking backward to see if he had hit the target, came up on the intercom.

"Major. The tail is on fire."

The U.S. Navy's riverine gunboat force early in the Vietnam conflict found many uses for helicopters. As shown here and on the two following pages, the riverine force called on the chopper for air cover, medevacuation, raking ambush sites and other gunfire support, even towing gunboats off of sandbars. The choppers also flew in supplies.

Sikorsky Skycranes ferried U.S. Navy river gunboats from stream to stream as the shifting action demanded.

Fire is the worst terror for helicopter crews, so Major Reilly set down immediately, though he was in enemy country. The crew deployed around the craft as a defense perimeter. Czomba ran to the rear to check the damage. The descent had snuffed out the flames, but fuel was spurting from tanks, completely soaking Czomba. Although he was a potential torch, Czomba ran through enemy fire across an open field to pluck several sticks from the tree line. He rammed them into the bullet holes and stopped the leaks, in time to save a meager 150 gallons. The crew stripped the chopper of all excess weight, dropping the heavy rocket pods, and Reilly started the engine. They had barely taken off when the VC charged, but the helicopter escaped. In the nearest friendly spot, Major Reilly set down. The engine coughed and died as the craft touched the ground.

The army gunship helicopters worked so well supporting navy riverine gunboat patrols that the navy borrowed eight of the craft and instructors to train pilots and enlisted gunners in gunship tactics. On October 26, 1966, the riverine force surprised a battalion-size crossing of Viet Cong on the Bassac River, about 50 miles below Can Tho. During the three-hour battle, gunboats and armed helicopters sank 50 of 75 enemy sampans and junks.

Meanwhile, a new tool for rescue and medical evacuation arrived in Vietnam. Designed by Kaman, the forest penetrator seat replaced finally the much-maligned sling. Pilots trying to winch casualties on the conventional sling had complained that the lift through dense jungle injured the wounded further. The new penetrator folded into a canvas-covered cylinder, a shape that easily slipped through the jungle roof. On the jungle floor, the wounded or a buddy removed the cover, then unfolded two seats and a shield. Two evacuees could mount simultaneously, grasp the shank, and give the thumbs-up signal, protected by the overhead shield. If the wounded soldier was hurt too bad, a paramedic descended to help him aboard the penetrator.

As late as 1967 helicopters were still lifting wounded by the primitive horsecollar sling. This wounded Marine is clinging firmly and his biceps are bulging, so he probably made it.

Two views, both from Sea Knights, of wounded Marines being readied for a lift by jungle penetrator. Rugged terrain and thick undergrowths prevented helicopter landings, leading to the specially designed hoists for picking up the wounded.

About the same time, the Viet Cong dreamed up a new dirty trick to make the medevac helicopter pilot's life unhappy. In late 1967, pilot Lt. (jg.) P. D. Cullen, copilot Lt. (jg.) L. L. Duncan, and crewmen G. D. Russell and R. R. Lavigne spotted the body of an American aviator in a rice paddy. The farmers nearby gestured to the fliers, indicating a peaceful intention to help. The suspicious pilot posted his crewmen at the guns and hovered over the body. When he saw the pilot was dead, he knew he was in a trap and banked away. About 40 VC opened fire from behind the paddy dikes. Cullen called in rocket strikes to work over the ambush area.

A new military helicopter application that had major importance for civilian life as well was the 273rd Army Aviation Company's use at Vung Tau of the new CH-54A—the Skycrane—as a longshoreman. During the last week of 1967, the craft, as ungainly looking as a praying mantis, began unloading cargo from the Australian troop transport H.M.A.S. *Sydney*. Major James E. Rogers as pilot, Maj. Gary R. Heffner as copilot, with crewmen Ramon Amaya, Jr., and Hartwell B. Wilson made history by unloading 304 tons of cargo in 4 hours, 34 minutes, a three-day job by conventional off-loading methods. The loads included three 3/4-ton Land Rovers rigged for a single lift and an 18,700-pound prime mover. Chinook helicopters from the 147th Assault Support Helicopter Company brought in troops of the First Australian Task Force. The transport left the same day it arrived. Freight handlers around the world took note.

Another medevacuation by a Sea Knight equipped with a special lifting device, this one of a Marine wounded in the so-called Demilitarized Zone.

Just after sunset, on January 5, 1968, a large North Vietnamese force ambushed a U.S. Army infantry company west of Tam Ky in South Vietnam. The enemy force was possibly battalion-size, and their firepower pounded the surrounded riflemen mercilessly, forcing them to draw in their perimeter throughout the night. Shortly after midnight, another infantry company came to their relief. Field medics reported that they were treating 40 wounded; several had been killed, and

more than 20 were missing. Medical supplies were running low, and the medics were taking hits while treating the casualties.

To save flight time once the helicopters could work, the division surgeon flew medical supplies to an advanced fire base and set up an emergency treatment center. At dawn two medevac helicopters from Maj. Patrick Brady's outfit loaded medical supplies for treatment of the wounded. One of the choppers was Brady's.

Speed in getting the wounded to a medevac helicopter for a lift to more sophisticated treatment than was available in the field saved uncounted lives—certainly several tens of thousands. These Marines have another reason for hurrying: in each instance, their buddies were hit by sniper fire. The chopper's landing "pad" is a potato patch, too close to the site of an enemy ambush.

Aboard a helicopter headed for the nearest hospital, a medevac crewman presses his thumb to the artery of Lance Corp. A. Ray to stop the bleeding from a gunshot wound in the arm.

Sikorsky Sea Kings trailing submarine detectors. Some of these devices work sonically, others magnetically. A trio of helicopters equipped with the detectors can pinpoint with deadly accuracy the location of a submerged submarine.

The embattled troops had cleared an area large enough for a UH-1, but a fog had socked in the area and they had no flares, only two grenades that gave off purple smoke. Major Brady took off several times but could not penetrate the fog. At 9:30 A.M., he could not stand any longer the thought of wounded waiting for rescue. He took off and circled slowly lower and lower through the fog, feeling for the trees. When the forest loomed through the haze, he used his downwash to blow a clear patch till he located a farm road. Listening to radio instructions from the infantrymen, he followed the road toward their position. First overshooting the area, he returned to find the purple smoke staining the fog.

Major Brady landed and unloaded medical supplies and flares as he took aboard six litters with wounded. The flares Major Brady had flown in guided the helicopters following. During the morning, Brady used three helicopters to bring out 51 of the wounded; two choppers were shot

A Sea Knight came into a hot zone of combat to pick up wounded Marines and crashed. Another Sea Knight lands to evacuate the stranded crew and their wounded passengers under covering fire of a Marine squad. Two Marines going to the rescue of the downed Marines are silhouetted against the burning craft.

out from under him. He won the Congressional Medal of Honor for his dogged insistence on penetrating the fog to save his comrades.

On January 21, 1968, began the Viet Cong attack on Khe Sanh, one of the pivotal battles of the war. The joint U.S. Marine-South Vietnamese outpost was dangerously vulnerable to isolation, and by early February enemy artillery fire had cut off Khe Sanh. General William C. Westmoreland decided to hold the strongpoint, supplying it by air.

During February, fog hugged the ground mornings till almost noon, then lifted to no more than 500 or so feet. Communists shelled the field from hills on either side of the approach. To foil the anti-aircraft fire, rear-unloading C-130 cargo planes came in at an unnaturally steep angle, turned off the runway to the ramp which ran parallel to the landing strip, dumped cargo while taxiing, turned back to the runway at the end of the taxiway, and took off. Passengers had

to get off or on at a dead run. Shellfire followed the plane the length of its unloading run.

Inevitably, a C-130 was hit on approach. The plane landed, but fire drove the pilot and the co-pilot out the overhead escape hatch. The cargo

A Boeing Vertol Sea Knight, hit on takeoff from the Phu Bai airstrip, caught fire and crashed. The helicopter's machine-gun ammunition was cooking off, and flames approached the fuel tanks. Fearful of an explosion, the pilot, two crewmen, and a passenger dragged the unconscious 1st Lt. Thomas Bowditch from the crash and carried him across a field to cover in the forest. Next morning they discovered they had crossed a minefield and, by all the rules of warfare, should have had their legs blown off.

To keep a mountaintop fire-support base supplied, a Sea Knight delivers ammunition for 105-mm. howitzers near Dong Ha in South Vietnam.

holds were loaded with bladder tanks of fuel, and seven passengers died when the plane exploded.

The C-130 pilots switched their unloading techniques. They hitched parachutes to loads mounted on wheeled pallets. Flying five feet over the runway, they popped the chutes out the rear cargo door, letting the drag pull the pallets out of the plane.

On March 6, 1968, one of the smaller C-123 fixed-wing aircraft was shot down on its landing approach. The 48 men aboard died.

The burden of evacuating the wounded and

Heavy-lift helicopters make possible swift deployment of even heavily armed troops. Here a Chinook is bringing in a 105-mm. howitzer.

delivering cargo too delicate for crash-unloading methods shifted to helicopters. After several helicopters were shot down, the Marines developed the tactic called Super Gaggle. Under that plan, transport helicopters flew with escorts of A-4 jet fighter-bombers and Huey gunships, the task force controlled by an airborne tactical air controller in a two-seat trainer version of the Skyhawk fighter-bomber. An aerial tanker hung about to refuel the fighter-bomber escort on station.

When weather predictions favored Super Gaggle, the air controller checked over the battle-field to be sure flying conditions were right, then called up the tankers, fighter-bombers, Huey gunships, and CH-46A heavy-lift helicopters.

Typically, the fighter-bombers worked over the area with napalm, rockets, and 20-mm. explosive machine-cannon shells. They laid smoke screens to blind the enemy. The CH-46 heavy-lifts dropped into Khe Sanh to unload cargo and pick up the wounded. Gunships followed them down to provide fire support or pick up the crew if a CH-46 crashed. During the operation of Super Gaggle, only two helicopters were shot down, and both of their crews were picked up by Huey escorts.

Despite the remoteness of the area, a Sea Knight enjoys the luxury of a wooden landing platform on a mountaintop only because other helicopters brought in the lumber.

During the Khe Sanh fight, the enemy attacked a Special Forces camp at Lang Vei. Hoping to draw a relief force from Khe Sanh, the enemy posted tanks with cannon zeroed in on all landing zones near the beleaguered outpost. Scouts reported that the enemy had overlooked an airstrip, about 1,600 feet east of the outpost perimeter. Alerted by radio, the camp's survivors sprinted for the strip, where CH-46s scooped them up. Gunships and jet planes blasted the surrounding zone. Nevertheless, three helicopters suffered hits. Captain Robert J. Richards' CH-46 was so overloaded he was having trouble clearing the trees. A North Vietnamese soldier stepped out of the jungle and sprayed the craft with an automatic rifle, tearing out the craft's instrument panel. The helicopter door gunner cut down the enemy sniper.

By March 15, 1968, action was slackening at Khe Sanh, and friendly mountain tribesmen reported that the North Vietnamese were pulling out. To encourage the withdrawal, Marines and South Vietnamese Rangers pressed attacks farther and farther from the defense perimeter. The North Vietnamese had been foiled in trying to reenact the French catastrophe at Dien-bien-phu, largely because the Americans had helicopter support and the French didn't.

Two minutes after a crash alert, U.S. Navy officers Lt. (jg.) Thomas L. Olson as pilot and Lt. John P. Meyer as copilot lifted off their Kaman Seasprite to rescue a pilot who had jumped from his plane. They were on the spot so fast they had to wait for the parachuting pilot to float down before they could pick him out of the sea.

One more reason why riding a helicopter beats walking.

The threat to Khe Sanh, coupled with the bloody Tet offensive, shook American confidence. President Johnson obliquely indicated he was not planning to escalate ground fighting. Cracks in the home front widened; resistance to the war increased.

In the post-Khe Sanh fighting, Capt. Arnie Reiner of the Marines, flying a CH-46A, descended to pick up eight wounded at the 2,400-foot level of a mountain two miles west of the relieved fortress. Mortars plowed up the landing zone on the steep mountainside. Captain Reiner withdrew to give the four escort gunships a chance to clean out opposition. Because the slope was so steep, on his return he had to lower a ramp with only the rear wheels touching the ground. Seven

stretcher bearers loaded the eight wounded and climbed aboard themselves. A mortar shell burst six feet from the craft, spraying the party with shrapnel. Captain Reiner used the slope to aid takeoff of his overloaded craft by diving to pick up air speed. Three mortar shells burst on the takeoff spot seconds after he left. At the base, mechanics counted 150 holes in the blades and fuselage.

During the night of June 19, 1968, the rescue-alert crew on the frigate U.S.S. *Preble* got word that a Phantom fighter was down 20 miles inland in North Vietnam. Lieutenant (jg.) Clyde E. Lassen with copilot Lt. (jg.) Clarence L. Cook and crewmen Bruce B. Dallas and Donald West took off in a Kaman Seasprite. As they neared the crash site, two Russian-built SAM missiles streaked by, leaving a trail of orange fire.

Lieutenant Lassen landed in a rice paddy about 200 yards from the flaming wreckage of the fighter plane, but ground fire drove him off. Escort planes dropped flares, and Lassen spotted the two airmen between trees about 50 yards apart. He hovered overhead while Lieutenant Dallas lowered the rescue seat. The flares guttered out, and Lassen lost his ground reference; the helicopter drifted in the darkness.

Dallas, who was leaning outside the craft attending his hoist, reported: "I started retracting the hoist as fast as possible, and in the process, the helo hit the tree on the right side. In my leaning out, I was also hit on the face as the tree went by. As soon as the limb hit me, I yelled 'Get up! Get up!' and we were out of there and climbing."

In an experiment to control Viet Cong infiltration of South Vietnam villages, U.S. armed forces evacuated civilians from broad areas, carrying the displaced villagers to refugee camps by helicopter. Two Marines improvised a stretcher to move a paralyzed man to the helicopter; another Marine carries an elderly woman.

Chief Hospital Corpsman Richard Felton shows the strain of sympathy for a young South Vietnamese, stricken with paralysis, being lifted out of a flooded village to a hospital.

On the lift-out, the craft hit the tree again and lurched into a sharp right turn. Something had been jarred loose, for the helicopter vibrated badly, but Lieutenant Lassen had become stubborn about the pickup. He radioed the survivors to head for a clearing and ordered his crewmen to shoot up the area. He tried landing but was driven off by gunfire. He flew closer to the running pilots and hovered low enough for them to crawl aboard while the gunners pounded the enemy gun nests. On the way to the coast, gunfire tore off a door. Vibration was shaking the craft so hard Lassen had to fight for control. Fuel drained away frighteningly. They landed on the U.S.S. *Jouett* with less than five minutes of fuel left. Lieutenant Lassen received the Congressional Medal of Honor, the first navy pilot to win the award in the Vietnam War. His copilot, Lieutenant Cook, won a Navy Cross, and crewmen Dallas and West received Silver Stars.

On another front, a parachuting fighter pilot floated into a canyon too deep for the 250-foot-long rescue hoist. He could not climb the sides of the canyon, for the Viet Cong were searching for him. By radio the rescue helicopter filled in the downed pilot on a ruse to draw away the enemy. The chopper flew out of sight behind the ridge closing in the canyon, unloaded a crewman in an orange flight suit, climbed above the ridge, and—in full view—lifted the crewman into the helicopter and flew off. The Viet Cong thought the chopper pilot had found and rescued their prey, so they left. The downed pilot climbed all night, and at dawn the helicopter returned to pick him up unmolested.

Over the beaches, enemy fire became doubly hot, for the Communists had installed Russian-built SAM missile batteries. They were knocking down the fastest jets. Their tactic against helicopters was to wait till they were straight overhead before opening fire.

Fighter pilot Lt. Comdr. D. A. Varich crashed only 30 miles south of Hanoi, the capital of North Vietnam. He hid on a cliff within hearing distance of a North Vietnamese Army training camp. Lieutenant Neil Sparks, piloting an SH-3A, with copilot Lt. (jg.) Robert Springer and crewmen Alvin L. Masengale and Teddy Ray hovered close to the navy flier's hideout on the cliffside, giving away the whole game. A storm of automatic fire broke out. The downed pilot jumped aboard, and the

Left: The U.S. Army made such yeoman use of helicopters, especially of heavy-lift models, during the Vietnam War that priority in assignment of tasks and equipment shifted steadily to the ground forces.

Top: Sea King helicopters landing on the carrier U.S.S. *Randolph* after antisubmarine exercises. Modern nuclear submarines can easily outrun the fastest surface ships, so the navy has become heavily dependent on helicopters for sonar detection and killing of enemy submarines with homing torpedoes. Bottom: A Sea King takes off from the *Randolph*. Warming up at the right of the picture is the propeller-driven S-2E plane for long-range scouting and tracking.

helicopter ran for the coast through a continuous anti-aircraft barrage. A SAM missile sailed by the craft and burst overhead. Lieutenant Sparks won the Navy Cross, and the others received Silver Stars.

Beach actions became increasingly horrendous. Going to the aid of an attack pilot, Lt. (jg.) Sam Payne crossed the beachline and then crashed under the fire of concealed batteries. He was hit in both hands and legs. His crew pulled him from the craft and blew it up. An air force HH-3E—the Jolly Green Giant—had been following the action and braved the fire to pick up all hands.

While trying to pick up two airmen in the water near an enemy-held island, a helicopter was hit by island batteries and crashed into the sea. Lieutenant William E. Terry, flying an SH-3A,

headed for the scene. Escorting attack planes warned him away, but he answered he could not abandon two aircraft crews. A pair of U.S. destroyers steamed between the shore batteries and the downed aviators. The ships pounded the island gun positions with a devastating fire. Aided by two other helicopters that came running, Lieutenant Terry picked up all the downed airmen. Most of them were severely wounded; two were dead.

Flying a small Kaman Seasprite, Lt. J. L. Meiling during one month picked up nine aviators in the dangerous offshore waters. When a Skyhawk pilot ditched off the North Vietnamese coast, Lieutenant Meiling made a slow pass over the site while crewman Allen E. Salsbury jumped into the water with an inflatable raft to pick up the flier.

Tough as they were, some helicopters did nevertheless crash. This Huey was photographed from the deck of the U.S.S. *Okinawa* just as it hit the water.

Marines rush a wounded Vietnamese to a waiting medevac helicopter. The ubiquitous elephant grass not only made the walking difficult but effectively concealed enemy ambushes, hence the rifles held at the ready and the look of strain on the face of the shouting platoon leader.

Marines cover the landing of a Sea Knight so it can lift out their wounded comrades.

A Sikorsky Sea Stallion of the U.S. Navy towing a magnetic minesweeper to demonstrate the newest use of helicopters in warfare.

Shore batteries opened up with increasingly accurate fire. Meiling called in air strikes, but the shore fire was getting so hot that Salsbury and the Skyhawk pilot abandoned the raft and swam to sea. They had been gone only seconds when a shell landed dead center on the raft. Lieutenant Meiling picked up the pair and carried them to the frigate U.S.S. *Fox*.

The stretcher being lifted out of the jungle by a Sea Knight carries a severely wounded enemy soldier abandoned by his comrades.

In the interior, helicopter tactics continued to evolve. Marines landed scout patrols deep in enemy country by CH-46 helicopters fitted with 120-foot-long ladders, six feet wide, so that the whole scout team could scramble to the ground during a low-flying pass. The choppers picked up the team the same way, stopping just long enough for the ground troops to grab a handhold and then flying off with the team dangling below. During the lift-out, escort gunships shot up the area. The long flight home at the bottom of a ladder curled many a Marine scout's hair with fright, but it beat getting shot during the slower conventional loading method.

The Coast Guard sent helicopter officers into combat in an exchange program with the U.S. Air Force. A Jolly Green Giant, piloted by Lt. Jack Rittichier of the Coast Guard, trying to pick up a downed Marine pilot west of Khe Sanh was hit, burst into flames, and crashed, killing all aboard. Rittichier and his crew were posthumously awarded Silver Stars.

Medevac helicopter crews were not above taking out a wounded scout dog. A booby trap wounded both the dog and his master, a Marine private.

On July 1, 1968, Lt. Col. Jack Modica of the air force ejected from his F-105 and landed in North Vietnam. For two days, helicopters and escorts tried to get to the pilot, who had an injured back, but ground fire drove off four rescue attempts. One Jolly Green Giant, piloted by Captain Oliver, with Major Stafford as copilot and crewmen Sgt. John Rodriguez and S. Sgt. James L. Miller, survived several hits from small-arms fire, but when a B-40 rocket lodged in a fuel tank, threatening to explode at any second and turn the craft into a flying fireball, Captain Oliver withdrew to get rid of his unwanted cargo. During this recovery effort, an escort fighter was shot down and the pilot killed, so the air commander called off the mission.

UH-34D helicopters surveying the deliberate firing of the jungle to clear off Hill 22 in South Vietnam during Operation Incinerator.

The army developed a scary method for lowering troops into the Vietnam jungle—or "inserting" them, as the military put it in their quaint jargon. To "extract" them, the helicopters hovered only long enough for the soldiers to grab a rung of the ladder and then flew them to a safe landing pad while they dangled in the air.

Before the fifth rescue attempt, B-52 bombers made a carpet strike nearby. A high-level carpet bombing is one of the most frightening experiences in warfare, and the rescue forces hoped the enemy would be shaken enough to permit another try. Lieutenant Lance Eagan of the Coast Guard and Maj. Bob Booth of the air force flew the primary rescue helicopter, with Sgt. Herbert H. Honer as flight engineer and Joel Talley as para-rescueman.

As they approached his position, the downed pilot touched off a smoke marker. Bursts of anti-aircraft cannon fire shook the craft, but Lieutenant Eagan maintained a hover while Talley descended on the forest penetrator to the jungle floor. He found the injured pilot some distance away, and Eagan had to move to within 30 feet of the pair, slicing off tree branches with his rotor blades. Talley strapped himself and Modica into the penetrator, and Lieutenant Eagan lifted out of gun range. At the Marine base at Dong Ha, mechanics reported the craft was so badly damaged it should not have been able to fly back from the pickup point. They would not certify it as fit to fly to its home base. Before an army Skycrane could pick up the craft and fly it home, Lieutenant Eagan in another helicopter with another crew picked up another fighter pilot, this time in the Gulf of Tonkin.

This Korean infantryman stepped on a poisoned stake during a search for Viet Cong. Snipers prevented the helicopter from landing, but the wounded Korean had no intention of being left behind.

In the fall of 1970, the Hoa An River ran in the full spate of a flash flood. The waters dropped a bridge into the stream; a truck loaded with South Vietnamese civilians dropped with it. They scrambled to the truck top, but rising waters threatened to carry them away. A Marine pilot, Ist Lt. Larry H. LaBrie, flying a CH-46, happened to be passing. He hovered beside the truck, and Sgt. David T. Howell dropped the side entrance door. The stranded natives were frightened of the aircraft, however, and refused to get aboard. Sergeant George E. Simons leaped to the truck and, in the best Marine manner, vigorously persuaded the shrinking natives to board.

In a war that baffled and frustrated the American military, the most frustrating effort occurred the night of November 20, 1970.

After darkness fell, a vast air armada from several U.S. services took off from bases in Thailand and on Okinawa and from carriers at sea and headed for North Vietnam on a mission bold enough to dazzle the most blasé of the warriors involved. They were working together to free the American prisoners of war held in a compound at Son Tay, just west of Hanoi. From Ta Khli in Thailand came a C-130 carrying the strike force. From Nakhon Phanom Royal Thai Air Force Base came close-support A-1E attack planes. From Udorn RTAFB came HC-130 tankers for in-flight refueling and six Phantom jets for anti-MIG high

Helicopters planning to unload troops in a landing zone are discouraged by pinpoint enemy artillery fire.

cover. From Korat RTAFB came five F-105 fighters for suppression of SAM missiles and anti-aircraft batteries and two EC-121 airborne command posts. From Kadena Airfield on Okinawa came an RC-135 carrying the airborne mission commander. From U-Tapao RTAFB came a KC-135 radio-relay aircraft. In the Gulf of Tonkin, carriers prepared to launch 60 navy fighter-bombers.

Most important of all—the heart of the operation—were six assault helicopters: five Super Jolly Green Giants (HH-53s) and one Jolly Green Giant (the smaller HH-3E), all heavily armed.

Problems developed even before takeoff. The C-130 that was to drop flares for the choppers could start only three of its four engines. The general commanding the operation gave permission for a three-engine flight. The fourth engine finally caught, but the trouble had thrown the plane 23 minutes behind schedule. As the helicopters took off from Udorn, some errant fighter pilot who hadn't got the word flew his plane straight through the formation, scattering Green Giants about the sky in their scramble to escape.

The assault force zigzagged to evade radar detection. As the airmen descended through the clouds into Red River Valley, they saw a magnificent scene. Major Frederic M. Donohue, piloting a Super Jolly Green Giant gunship, reported:

"Ahead the lights of Hanoi were beautiful. And just beyond them, the navy planes had the

To take the high ground has always been a basic infantry tactic. Helicopters in South Vietnam airlifted Marines to mountaintop positions unreachable by foot.

Atop the Rock Pile, four miles south of the Demilitarized Zone in Vietnam, Marine lookouts control a half-dozen trails used by the North Vietnamese. So steep were the slopes that supply helicopters could land only one wheel at a time.

Helicopters are deadly foes of the submarine, but they cannot work alone. They search and attack in company with destroyers and long-range tracking aircraft. Submarines, submerged or on the surface, are also involved in the antisubmarine training exercises shown here.

Right, top: The draft mule of the Vietnam War was the U.S. Marines' version of the Boeing Vertol Chinook, a heavy-lift helicopter that could absorb incredible punishment and still fly. Right, bottom: Originally meant for reconnaissance and light utility only, the chopper proved a formidable weapons platform in combat. Here shown firing a ripple of small rockets, the chopper becomes a deadly tank killer when armed with TOW missiles.

A wounded Marine on his way to a waiting medevac helicopter.

sky over Haiphong harbor lit up like the Fourth of July with flares. There was an awful lot of commotion, and there must have been a lot of noise."

The navy diversion worked, for the assault force reached Son Tay undetected. At 2:30 A.M., the C-130 dropped its flares. The lead helicopter sailed over the prison camp walls, shattering guard towers with gunfire. The chopper following landed in a clearing, smashing its way through a giant tree on the way down.

"We tore into it like a big lawnmower," said Col. Herb Zehnder, copilot. "There were limbs,

brush, branches, and leaves everywhere. That tree must have been 150 feet tall, much higher than we thought. There was a tremendous vibration, the rotor system was damaged, and we were down."

The third helicopter unloaded the assault riflemen—unfortunately, at the wrong compound. They reloaded and took off, found the right compound, and landed again. The next chopper came in according to plan. The other two stood by on river islands eight miles away as a backup rescue force in case the assault helicopters were damaged.

Interservice support among helicopter and related units reached its peak in Vietnam. The bareheaded warrior shown leading the stretcher bearers is U.S. Navy corpsman "Doc" Fred E. Davis, assigned to a Marine medevac helicopter squadron.

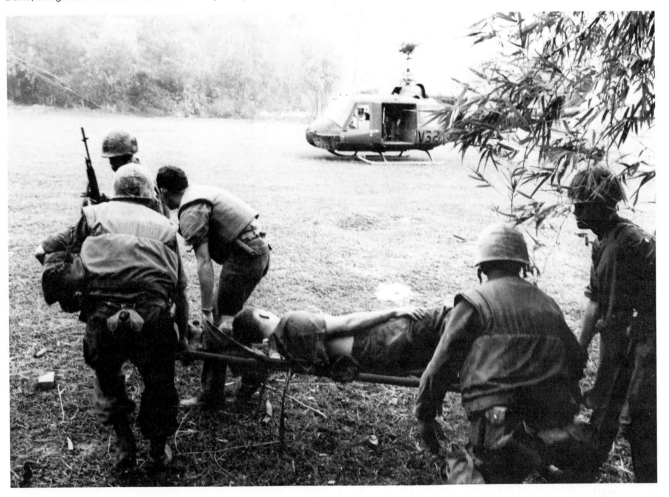

In August 1965, during Operation Starlight, embattled Marines urgently called for medevac help. Though a firefight was raging within 50 yards of the pickup zone, helicopters dropped in and took out the fallen Marines.

At the Son Tay compound, the army volunteers from the Special Forces group raged through the buildings, knocking down doors, shooting down North Vietnamese, and raising general hell. To little effect, for—incredibly—nobody was home. No prisoners of war anyhow. The place had ceased to be a prison camp some time before, and the vast and complicated machinery of the raid had been grinding away at nothing.

The North Vietnamese were recovering from their surprise. SAM missiles began zapping all over the sky like flying telephone poles. MIGs would be along any minute. After 27 minutes on the ground, the assault force left. The force suffered only two casualties: one of the raiders broke an ankle, another had a gunshot wound in the thigh.

The fiasco caused an uproar in the States. But nobody blamed the warriors involved. They had

In-air administration of plasma to this wounded Marine probably saved another of the thousands of lives snatched from death by speedy helicopter evacuation. The corpsman is ''Doc'' Fred E. Davis.

A Sikorsky Sea Stallion towing a magnetic minesweeping device about the waters of Haiphong harbor in North Vietnam in 1973 as part of the closing down of American participation in the Indochinese conflict.

done their part with exquisite precision. Had the prisoners been where military intelligence said they were, those helicopters would have brought them home. Anybody who has ever been in combat will verify that Son Tay was not the first failure of military intelligence, or the last.

Even the failure of the mission gave the enemy—and the world—something to think about. The helicopter had become a formidable battle weapon indeed.

Late in the war, ordnance experts experimentally equipped helicopters with tubes housing TOW missiles (tube-launched, optically tracked, wire-guided missiles), and the aircraft went tank hunting. The record of those experimental missile ships, even in the few days of fighting left to them, established firmly that the helicopter is the most effective antitank weapon in the army's arsenal. Today all battle planning includes the helicopter as the mainstay of defense against tank attack.

After the cease-fire of January 27, 1973, the services began the study of battle actions to discover what had happened.

Among the servicemen awarded the Congressional Medal of Honor in Vietnam were several from the helicopter force. Some, but by no means all, of the men and their stories follow.

Chief Warrant Officer Frederick E. Ferguson on January 31, 1968, volunteered to take a UH-1

A helicopter fights a fire in downtown Saigon, South Vietnam, by dumping tons of water on the
burning buildings.

into the heart of the enemy-occupied city of Hue to rescue the crewmen and wounded passengers of a helicopter that had been shot down into a hornet's nest of enemy firepower. He landed on a postage-stamp-size clearing in the rubble, blowing up a dense cloud of dust. Mortar and machine-gun fire riddled his craft, but he flew out the stranded survivors of the crash.

First Lieutenant James P. Fleming on November 26, 1968, held his Huey against a riverbank with the tail over the water while a Special Forces patrol mounted the craft under intense enemy fire. He held steady, though his fuel was nearly exhausted and the windshield was carried away in a shower of splinters by machine-gun bullets.

Major Stephen W. Pless on August 19, 1967, while flying an escort mission in a gunship, intercepted an emergency call for help from four Americans boxed in on the beach and under attack by a large Viet Cong force. He surprised the enemy, carving the VC to tatters as they fled for the tree line. Major Pless then put his gunship between the Americans and the enemy as a shield while his crewmen loaded the wounded men aboard. Although his craft was so overloaded that it touched the water four times before he could get it aloft, Major Pless brought the soldiers home.

Private First Class Gary G. Wetzel on January 8, 1968, was door gunner on a Huey trapped in a landing zone by heavy enemy fire. He was blown into a rice paddy by two rocket blasts. Ignoring the loss of his left arm and other wounds, he climbed back to his gun and silenced the enemy gun emplacements.

Sergeant Rodney J. T. Yano on January 1, 1969, suffered partial loss of his sight and the use of one arm when a phosphorous grenade accidentally burst inside his helicopter. Although he was covered with the blazing chemical, he jettisoned flaming ammunition to save the rest of the crew, burning himself still more grievously. He died, and was awarded the medal posthumously.

Hundreds of other helicopter warriors per-

Vietnamese helicopters bringing out military men and their
families after Saigon fell to the Communists had to be pushed
over the side or ditched to make room for following craft. The
U.S.S. *Blue Ridge* alone dumped 15 helicopters into the sea.

With no place to land his chopper, this South Vietnamese pilot jumps out and ditches it near the
U.S.S. *Blue Ridge.*

This Chinook heavy-lift helicopter has left the Vietnam scene, but the three water buffalo are still there plugging away.

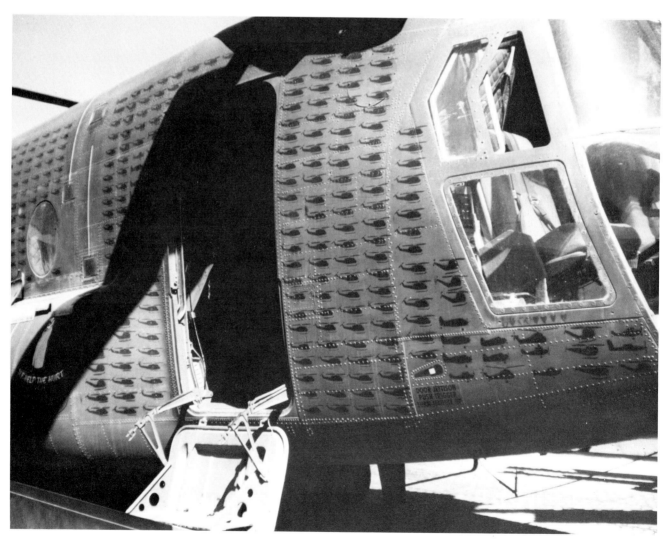

The symbols on this veteran helicopter represent the chopper's rescues and salvage operations in the Vietnam conflict.

formed deeds of valor worthy of the highest award, deeds that went more or less unnoticed in the welter of heroic acts that became almost commonplace.

What drove those flesh-and-blood human beings to superhuman deeds? Perhaps there is something about the whickering rhythm of the rotor blades, a rhythm that matches the heartbeat, making the machine seem an extension of the man. Maybe the swooping lift-off pumps adrenalin into the blood. The unlovely machines do something to their crews, for no branch of the service distinguished itself so much as the helicopter force for selfless service and breathtaking courage.

As for what the helicopters accomplished in Vietnam.... Battle effectiveness of the gunships and TOW antitank aircraft aside, the helicopters rescued 93 percent of the crews of all the downed aircraft they went after, more than 50 percent of those downed behind enemy lines. They doubled the odds for survival of wounded over the Korean record, itself a vast improvement over previous wars. Indeed, because of quick helicopter evacuation, a wounded soldier in Vietnam had a 41 percent better chance of survival than an automobile crash victim in the United States.

And the chopper turned out to be not nearly so vulnerable as first feared. Out of some 760,000 combat missions flown a helicopter was hit once in 325 combat sorties, shot down once in 6,400 sorties, and shot up beyond recovery and repair once in 13,000 sorties.

6

New Civilian Uses

The Louisiana Wildlife and Fisheries Commission, one of the nation's most progressive conservation agencies, in 1963 embarked on a program to establish a statewide deer herd by restocking barren areas. Under the supervision of Richard Yancey and Allan Ensminger, federal and state game experts trapped deer from overbrowsed ranges on federal and state refuges. They selected healthy does and young bucks, rejecting old males as useless for building new herds. The 104 selects were loaded on a Bell 47G-2A of Petroleum Helicopters, Incorporated, piloted by A. C. Davenport, and transferred to northern parishes where good browsing existed but deer to enjoy it did not. With the help of helicopter transportation out of the marsh refuges, the cost of the operation was held to only $10 a head.

The same year, in southwestern Washington, hemlock loopers threatened 70,800 acres of prime timber—and incidentally $40 million in payrolls. Looper reproduction in the spring of 1963 outstripped the ability of the pest's natural enemies, such as birds and other insects, to keep the population within tolerable limits. Two and three million worms to the acre stripped the hemlocks bare of needles. The owners of the threatened timber—the United States, the State of Washington, the Weyerhaeuser Company, the Crown-Zellerbach Corporation, and 100 minor owners—united behind the Willapa Hemlock Looper Control Project.

Supervising the operation were more than 60 experts from forest services, fisheries departments, pollution-control agencies, chemical companies, sportsmen's groups, and the commercial oyster growers of Willapa Bay.

The Helicopter Services Company of Yakima, Washington, and the Vertex Helicopter Company of Chehalis, Washington, flew in 14 machines, most of them Bell 47Gs. Spraying crews had to wait for fair weather, so rain would not wash away the mix of Sevin and bacillus pesticide before it could do in the varmints. On July 5, 1963, the sun rose hot and bright in a clear sky, and the helicopters took off. Up to nine choppers at a time sprayed four hours a day, usually in the morning to escape afternoon high winds. By July 31, 1963, the job was done.

Entomologists reported a 95 percent kill of loopers; biologists reported no damage to fish or wildlife and credited helicopter precision application for the operation's success.

The Florida Game and Fresh Water Fish Commission tracked poachers in the vast Everglades and Big Cypress Swamp wilderness with a Bell 47G-2. Tracks of swamp buggies and crawlers, even tracks of airboats, are clearly visible from the air, and the helicopter can follow them to where intruders are taking deer out of season or killing alligators for their hides. The helicopter also transports wild turkeys in burlap bags lashed to the floats for restocking barren forests.

Application of pesticide by a Hiller 12E to kill the hemlock looper infesting forests in southwestern Washington was so precise that the vulnerable oyster beds of Willapa Bay, at the top of the picture, escaped damage.

In New Zealand, a Bell 47G-3B does another kind of conservation work by thinning out herds of imported whitetail deer that threaten to strip the mountainsides of protective tree cover by overbrowsing. Peter Anisy reports on the technique.

"On the venison recovery, we take the door off the passenger's side of the helicopter and shoot the deer while hovering above them. Then we hook the deer underneath the chopper and fly them to the roadside, where they are hung to cool before being taken by truck to the freezers."

Anisy also uses his helicopter to lower crawfish traps into the sea and pick them up the next day. He reports that both ventures pay a fine profit.

A Hiller demonstrates the precision spraying possibilities of the helicopter by hugging the ground at a 7,000-foot elevation.

A Bell 47G-2A piloted by Bob Schellinger and a Bell 47G-3B flown by Mel Callaway in 26 flying hours corraled 11,165 elk in Yellowstone National Park. The pilots kept the herd moving by kicking up artificial blizzards with the helicopters' downwash. Once the animals were inside the fences, the pilots landed and closed the gates. The elk had outgrown and overbrowsed their range. Authorities decided to corral them when the original plan, to thin the herd by shooting 5,000, stirred up a storm of protest.

The Kern River valley's rugged landscape makes it the ideal site for location shots of western movies. It also makes it a construction man's nightmare. Delivery of the structural steel beams to be used in building the Cow Creek flume for the Southern California Edison Company posed a bit of a problem, which was solved by using a rotary-wing craft to bring the steel beams across the ravines and mountains too rough even for mules.

On March 23, 1965, the Coast Guard cutter *Intrepid* took station east of Bermuda near the calculated splashdown center for the Gemini 3 spaceflight. The cutter *Diligence* took station 48 miles west of the *Intrepid*, and the *Vigilant* another 35 miles farther west. The capsule splashed down 45 miles short of the *Intrepid*. Lieutenant Commander Frederick Schubert, flying an HH-52A from the *Diligence*, found the capsule within 20 minutes. An air force C-54 dropped a pair of pararescue divers. One jumper landed near the target, but the diver with the vital flotation collar landed almost a mile away. The helicopter headed for the off-target swimmer but was ordered to stay clear. Some officials criticized the order, for it delayed the always tricky recovery of the capsule and its passengers, Virgil I. Grissom and John W. Young.

Among other curiosities of the stupendous Grand Canyon is the difference in climate between the South Rim and the North Rim, only four to 18 miles apart. The South Rim is a desert. The nearest water hole is a meager spring 3,000 feet down the canyon wall. The much higher North Rim has an almost Canadian climate and enjoys abundant water. But the South Rim is the easy one to get to, so tourists flock there and neglect the equally picturesque north side. At great expense, park officials had to haul in water to the South Rim by truck or tank car. The obvious solution was to pipe in some of the water from across the way. The National Park Service asked for bids to lay a four-mile pipeline but exacted such rigid restrictions that most contractors were frightened away.

None of the canyon's natural beauty was to be marred, and none of the vegetation was to be damaged. The contractor had to work within the limits of the Kaibab Trail, a 12.4-mile path only three feet wide in places and running across eight miles of solid rock. Any boulder dislodged had to be hoisted back in place. The Kaibab Trail descends into the canyon in a series of hairpin switchbacks, putting severe demands on pipe-laying machinery restricted to a narrow path.

In 1962 Elling Halvorson had contracted to

Deep snows in Norway one winter forced the Norwegian navy to press helicopters into service for weeks as school buses for 33 rural children.

build a microwave site atop 9,000-foot Echo Summit in California's High Sierras. In an area so rough that he had to haul in water to mix concrete, Halvorson finished the job with helicopters. Armed with that experience, he and Harold D. Lent, a pipeline expert, spent a month in the canyon—riding mules, walking the Kaibab Trail, and flying one of Halvorson's helicopters over the route. The Halvorson-Lent bid of $2.5 million won the pipeline contract.

Beginning at a gushing spring near the 5,000-foot level on the North Rim, the route ran along Bright Angel Creek, across the Colorado River on the canyon floor, and up the south wall to Indian Gardens, where it was to meet the existing pipeline. The contractors hired a retired navy flier, Lloyd Tracy, as chief helicopter pilot and began assembling equipment and supplies on the South Rim at Yaki Point. The chopper pilots shuttled between various job sites, including a base camp in Bright Angel Canyon to which they carried generators, a water system with showers, and prefabricated buildings.

Helicopters carried two 50-foot sections of pipe at a time. On a ledge 3,000 feet down the

The Union Pacific Railroad had contracted with a helicopter pilot to dust the right-of-way with weed killer. A radio call warned him that an express train, the City of Los Angeles, was on its way. "Just a little more to do," he answered—and was brought down by the train.

A Bell of Evergreen Helicopters picks up a load of water for fighting a forest fire.

To build a cable-car system across the harbor at Singapore from Mount Faber to the island of Sentosa, a Bell JetRanger laid 2.2 miles of nylon rope between three 200-foot-high poles. The cars carry 720 passengers an hour.

canyon wall, the contractors built a pipe bender for shaping lengths to fit curves along the route, and choppers flew the curved sections to the appropriate switchback on the trail. Four helicopters kept busy staying ahead of the ground work force; the entire pipeline project required some 25,000 round trips from rim to floor to haul approximately 15 million pounds of cargo.

In California's Angeles National Forest, helicopters were pressed into a grimmer kind of canyon duty on the night of November 1, 1966. They had been fighting a brush fire in Pacoima Canyon all day, moving men and tools, laying hose, and dropping thousands of gallons of fire retardant. Fire fighters from El Cariso Ranger Station in nearby Cleveland National Forest joined in to battle flames that fed on brush dried by a 100-degree heat wave. At sunset, a strong wind sprang up, with gusts to 50 miles per hour. Sparks and flaming branches blown downwind leapfrogged a party of fire fighters and trapped them inside a flaming ring. Helicopter pilot Roland Barton of the Los Angeles County Fire Department described the rescue operation.

"With dusk coming on and the smoke so thick, it was actually dark. There was no chance to land, due to the steep terrain. . . ."

A machine of Arizona Helicopters, Incorporated, piloted by Troy Cook, and another of the Los Angeles Sheriff's Department, piloted by Lt. Lyndell Griggers, joined the rescue effort. Ten of the ground crew had already died by the time they arrived, and so the choppers hovered, the blades in danger of clipping rocks uphill on the steep slope. They pulled up a dozen fire victims with second- or third-degree burns, all in critical condition. The helicopters brought in a medical team and 20 rescue volunteers. They carried out the 10 bodies in litters attached to the landing gear.

Working as a team, two helicopters drop a mudlike fire retardant at the rate of a ton every five minutes—11 times the weight of one of the machines in an hour—to combat a 74-square-mile forest fire on Oxbow Ridge in Oregon. The craft, belonging to Evergreen Helicopters, Incorporated, of McMinnville, Oregon, delivered twice as much retardant as conventional craft at one-third the cost and with 94 percent accuracy.

A Bell helicopter aids ground fire fighters in battling a brush blaze by dropping hundreds of pounds of fire suppressant over the area.

Robert Lee Hartman of an air development navy squadron's parachute rescue team packs his chute after making a practice jump from a Sea Horse helicopter to the Antarctic plateau near Williams Field. Since their first use in Antarctica during Operation High Jump in 1946, helicopters have become indispensable for exploration of polar regions.

Barton continued: "Between these operations, another crew got into trouble, and our fire department and Angeles National Forest helicopters proceeded to drop a great deal of retardant to cool off their line. We used straight water in 105-gallon tanks under the helicopters."

Demonstrating their invulnerability to bad weather, helicopters were the only vehicles moving in Chicago when, in January 1967, a blizzard dumped a record-breaking 23 inches of snow on the city and, after a short break, another 10 inches. Pressed into emergency service were helicopters from the city fire department, Chicago Helicopter Airways, Helicopter Air Lift, the U.S. Navy, and privately owned craft from the Hinsdale and Palwaukee airports. They landed anywhere—in parking lots, streets, and backyards and on riverbanks. They flew blood, drugs, pacemakers, and insulin to hospitals and food and supplies to housebound families. Engineers from the power and gas companies located broken lines, and repair crews arrived by helicopter. Newspapers carried banner headlines celebrating the versatility and toughness of the rotary-wing aircraft.

The U.S. Navy showed the power of a new generation of helicopters when a CH-53A towed a 500-foot ship displacing 16,000 tons, the two vehicles making 20 knots.

Three Bell UH-1D Iroquois helicopters of the type that made the first landing at the South Pole come in for refueling on Byrd Glacier in Antarctica.

In Tok, Alaska, during a bitter cold January, ice had built up eight inches thick around transmission wires and threatened to bring them down for miles around. An H-21 hovered over the lines to let the downwash sway them till the ice cracked off.

Near San Diego, California, Boatswain's Mate 1st Class Joseph Thrift, a sky diver with an underwater demolition team, jumped from a Boeing Vertol Sea Knight helicopter piloted by Lt. (jg.)

Bill Erickson. Thrift did a free-fall for 10,000 feet and popped his chute at 2,500 feet. It tangled in its own suspension lines and swelled into a "Mae West," a double-bulged clutter of cloth that gives virtually no drag. Thrift popped his reserve chute. It tangled with the "Mae West." Before horrified shipmates, he crashed to earth on his back.

Pilot Erickson had chased him down in autorotation at 130 knots. To the astonishment of everybody—perhaps to Thrift most of all—the sky diver was alive. Thrift was loaded into his jump helicopter for a medevac ride to a hospital, where he was treated for minor spinal fractures and bruises.

The New York City Environmental Protection Administration has used a helicopter to locate unmetered swimming pools using excessive water at no cost. It found more than 12,000 pools in backyards or on roofs in the borough of Staten Island alone. Officials expect the helicopter to ferret out 200,000 freeloaders.

The Russian fish-processing ship *Trubobaja Slava,* working 175 miles off Cape Cod, Massachusetts, in July 1967, radioed the U.S. Coast Guard that a waitress aboard had just given birth to a premature baby who was in danger because the ship had no incubator. The ship was beyond the round-trip range of the Coast Guard's HH-52As, so the cutter *Vigilant* raced to sea with an HH-52A aboard. When the *Vigilant* came within helicopter flight range of the Russian ship, Lt. William Solley took off with Lt. (jg.) George Ellis and crewman

In 1969 Rotorways of Phoenix, Arizona, was producing the Scorpion, a single-seater capable of sports cruising at 65 miles per hour and climbing to 12,000 feet.

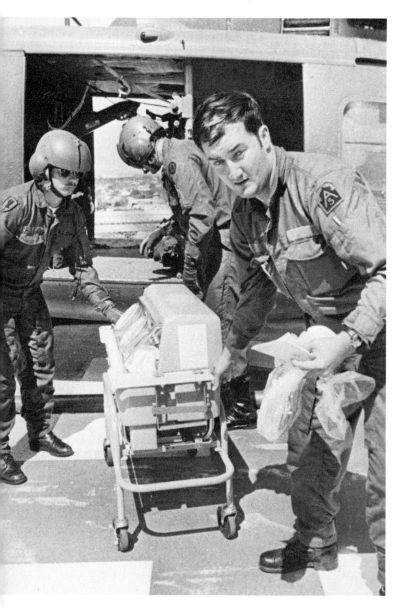

The U.S. Army has deployed 16 units nationwide in a program to give swift mobility in traffic and health emergencies. Called MAST, an acronym for Military Assistance to Safety and Traffic, the army's helicopters are particularly effective in rushing prematurely born babies to hospitals in specially designed mobile incubators, as in this operation at Santa Rosa, Texas.

Richard Martin. The chopper also carried a Public Health Service doctor and a portable incubator.

Language difficulty threatened to foul up the operation. The helicopter hovered over the ship and lowered the incubator to the deck in a basket, the flight crew expecting the Russians to put the incubator with the baby in it back into the basket so they could rush the infant ashore. Instead, the Russians unhooked the basket and took it below. The pilot sent down a note directing the sailors to put the baby in the basket. With the maddeningly uncooperative manner familiar to anybody who has had to deal with Soviet officials, the Russian captain insisted that the helicopter land on the ship, as though he were in charge of the rescue and doing the helicopter crew a favor.

"I didn't want to do it," Lieutenant Solley said. "It was dense fog, and there were masts and booms all around." For the sake of the baby, he did it. After landing he noted he had two feet of clearance for his rotors.

With the baby (in the incubator) and mother finally aboard, Solley took off straight up to clear the masts squeezing him in and flew back to the *Vigilant* for refueling. The next leg of the flight carried the baby and mother to the mainland. Inevitably, they had to go through the formalities, both immigration and customs clearance, but the officials moved faster than usual, and the pair reached Boston City Hospital in time to save the baby.

That same month of July 1967, at Annapolis, Maryland, a navy helicopter made a hospital run with young Bruce Taylor, who was suffering from gangrene. Antibiotics were not working. Doctors said the only treatment that could save the boy's leg was a high concentration of oxygen forced into the bloodstream by a hyperbaric oxygenation chamber. The nearest machine was five hours away by ambulance at New York City's Mount Sinai Hospital. A navy helicopter carried the boy in 1 hour, 15 minutes to a landing in Central Park, across the street from the hospital. Less than two weeks later, Bruce walked out on his own power, carrying a model of the navy chopper given to him by its designer, the famed Igor Sikorsky, who always rejoiced in a rescue mission performed by helicopter.

This Bell helicopter was forced by the rough terrain to hover while rescuers lifted aboard a seriously injured girl who had fallen on the rocks.

A Chinook heavy-lift helicopter transports a component for one of the lunar spaceflight vehicles.

Migrating ducks in Kings County, California, persisted in landing on a polluted pond faster than wardens could drive them off. Major Edwin G. Flanigen of the air force and Comdr. Ralph F. Bennie of the navy hovered over the pond in an H-21, frightening the ducks off, then chased them far enough downrange so they would not attempt a return.

In still another rescue and hospital run in July 1967, only the ingenuity of the chopper pilot made the pickup possible. Joe Savage, of Petroleum Helicopters, had just landed on an offshore oil platform in the Marsh Island area of Louisiana when he heard of a serious fire on a nearby platform. He took off and spotted three men in a life raft close to a rapidly spreading surface fire. Just then, an oil storage tank exploded, throwing flames 600 feet high and pushing the surface fire still faster toward the raft.

Savage landed on the water, and his passenger, oil company supervisor Hale B. Ingram, crawled out on a float to pull one man aboard. Flames threatened to drive off the rescue craft and engulf the raft till Savage changed the pitch of the blades, setting them to blow back the fire. Once the three men were aboard, he raced for the hospital at Morgan City, Louisiana, with a refueling stop on the way. From the first alarm to delivery of the three injured men at the hospital— including the refueling time—the rescue took 55 minutes.

The Sea King No. 66 drops flotation gear to swimmers during the pickup of astronauts James A. Lovell, Jr., and Edwin E. Aldrin, Jr.

The drill tower where Chicago firemen take courses in helicopter tactics stands on the spot where in 1871 Mrs. O'Leary's cow kicked over a lantern to start the Great Chicago Fire.

The U.S. Navy and the oil companies working offshore rigs abandoned the dangerous horsecollar sling after the reasonably safe lift device called a Billy Pugh net became available. Named for its designer, the device comes in several shapes and sizes; it may be a simple net, a chairlike conveyance holding one or two persons, or a large bell-shaped, cagelike basket capable of carrying four or more. On October 22, 1968, an SH-3A from the U.S.S. *Essex*, 285 miles south of Bermuda, picked up Walter M. Schirra, Jr., Donn F. Eisele, and R. Walter Cunningham on completion of the Apollo 7 flight, after 163 orbits of the earth. The helicopter used a Billy Pugh basket, and the operation went with unprecedented smoothness.

Apollo 8, the first spacecraft to orbit the moon, landed before sunrise near Christmas Island in the South Pacific on December 27, 1968. Aboard were James A. Lovell, Jr., Frank Borman, and William A. Anders. They splashed down only 7,100 yards from the U.S.S. *Yorktown*. The primary recovery helicopter, the Sea King No. 66, piloted by Comdr. Donald S. Jones, with backup and photography choppers standing by, was ready for instant pickup. The capsule floated so well, however, that the astronauts decided to stay buttoned up till daylight. They exchanged jokes and small

The Sea King No. 66 during recovery exercises for the Apollo 11 flight in July 1969 that put the first man on the moon.

talk with the helicopter crew. When the sky lightened 45 minutes after splashdown, para-rescue divers Lt. (jg.) Richard J. Flanagan and Seaman 1st Class Don Swab (what a great name for a sailor) fixed a flotation collar to the capsule and opened the hatch. Frogman Bob Crawford attached a sea anchor to the capsule to steady its bobbing and cut down the drift. The astronauts stepped out to a rubber raft and rose one at a time in a Billy Pugh net. It was the first of many space recoveries helicopter No. 66, a Sikorsky SH-3A, would make.

A victim's-eye view of a Billy Pugh basket being lowered from a Sea King. This picture was taken during practice rescues for the Apollo 10 mission. The pickup of the astronauts following the actual spaceflight was made by old faithful, Sea King No. 66.

Astronauts Richard F. Gordon, Jr., Charles Conrad, Jr., and Alan L. Bean practice a water pickup in preparation for the second lunar landing aboard Apollo 12 in November 1969.

In Montana a veterinary hospital maintains a heliport for the flying doctor who brings in animals strapped in litters outside his helicopter.

On Thursday, August 14, 1969, near Grand Cayman Island in the Caribbean Sea, observers spotted the first ominous signs of a spiral pattern in local winds. Slowly the winds built the speed of their rotation about a center that moved northwest at 10 miles per hour. By Friday evening, the disturbance had passed over the tip of Cuba into the Gulf of Mexico. Its winds had increased to official hurricane level, and the storm was named Camille. On Saturday afternoon, the storm stalled off the Florida coast and steadily beefed up its whirling force to a frightening 150 miles per hour. After dark Camille began moving again, toward Biloxi, Mississippi.

Early Sunday an air force hurricane-hunter plane crossed the eye of the storm and recorded a barometric pressure of 26.61 inches, the lowest ever recorded by a weather plane in the Western Hemisphere.

The Coast Guard at New Orleans, already

Coast Guard helicopters along the Gulf of Mexico scour the sea and marshes along the coast to warn boaters and trappers of an approaching hurricane.

Following Hurricane Inez in 1966, U.S. Navy and Marine helicopters land on a beach in the Dominican Republic. For those who have never witnessed the fury of a hurricane, the debris in this picture will bear witness, for half of it is parts of shattered homes.

warned of the hurricane's path, had called in additional helicopters from nearby stations and began rescue operations Sunday morning.

Major John A. Firse of the air force, on loan to the Coast Guard in an officer-exchange program, made the first rescue. Patrolling the forward edge of the storm, Firse intercepted a cry for help on the international distress frequency. The tug *Charlotte*, with a barge in tow, was sinking in the Gulf of Mexico, 70 miles southeast of New Orleans. Shortly after midnight, Major Firse found the tug and asked the skipper if he wanted a pump.

"No. I can't pump out the Gulf of Mexico. I'm going to beach it."

Major Firse stayed close and in radio contact.

"The captain was afraid that his engines would become flooded, and he would start drifting without lights or directional control. But he wanted to beach the boat and the barge in a spot that wouldn't block channels. He knew many boats would be using them to escape the hurricane."

Winds had increased to 60 miles per hour, and seas ran up to 25 feet high.

"That skipper sure had guts," said Major Firse. "He could have come off the boat at any time, but he stayed with it until he found the beach. The boat was listing badly and was lying over on its side by the time he beached it. The rest was easy. We hoisted the captain and five crewmen into the helicopter and brought them to New Orleans."

The barge survived, but the tug disappeared in the storm.

Camille hit the coast at Waveland, Mississippi, near the Louisiana border. Winds that probably reached 200 miles per hour, high tides up to 30 feet above normal, and what must have been hundreds of tornadoes smashed the delta of the Mississippi River and the Mississippi Gulf Coast with the most powerful blow of any storm in North American history.

The low-lying marshlands in the Mississippi Delta south of New Orleans had suffered several devastating storms, but Camille surpassed in fury anything that even those storm-weary coastal dwellers had seen. Stout buildings simply blew away piece by piece around the ears of those who had not fled. One young man, exposed to the full rage of the wind when his house disintegrated around his head, found himself dazed and half-drowned in the top of a tree. He did not remember climbing it and assumed he was blown there instead of into the raging tide where many of his neighbors died.

Along the Mississippi coast from Waveland to Biloxi, churches, supermarkets, antebellum mansions, motels, nightclubs, century-old live oak trees, pine forests—everything blew away.

In Mississippi a certain social level traditionally greets catastrophe with a party. Drought killing the cotton? Let's have a drought party. Too much rain? Let's have a rain party. So 21 death-defying

The Marines' caption material on their release of this 1970 photograph reports that the people peering into the chopper are victims of Typhoon Joan on Luzon Island in the Philippines. Which just proves how resilient the Filipinos are, for this group looks more like a crowd watching a Punch-and-Judy show, and a rather merry one at that.

revelers had gathered in a strongly built modern apartment complex for a hurricane party. They all drowned.

When the winds roared inland (to work terrible devastation in Virginia before the hurricane died), helicopters began arriving from military installations all over the southeastern states. They crisscrossed the skies carrying medical teams, food, drugs, blood, the injured to hospitals, and the stranded to dry land. For two days, they offered virtually the only transport on the Mississippi Gulf Coast and the delta country. Eventually bulldozers cleared the highways, and emergency repairs put bridges and causeways back in service. But it was the helicopter that kept the Gulf Coast country alive in the first weeks after Hurricane Camille.

A Pennsylvania State Highway Police helicopter spotted a motorist dumping a huge load of trash beside a lonely highway. The pilot hovered over the scene. The driver gathered the scattered trash and put it back in his car. No conversation. No ticket.

Left, top: Helicopters once flew tourists on sight-seeing trips over Paris and surrounding France, and the service may be resumed with the availability of new, more powerful craft. Left, bottom: A Bell 212 hovers over London, England.

Far out in the Pacific in early January 1970, 50-foot waves swept over French Frigate Shoals, inundating the loran station on one of the islands. When the storm passed, the island, which is little more than a sandbar, remained under three feet of water. The station was out of commission and the crew stranded atop the power plant. A helicopter from the Royal New Zealand Navy frigate *Waikato* carried the survivors to safety.

On June 9, 1970, a U.S. Army chopper pilot, flying relief services in a Boeing Vertol Chinook after an earthquake in Peru, found a mountain village where nobody had eaten in days. The pilot

Fifty-pound sacks of wheat being delivered to victims of Typhoon Joan in the Philippines by Sea Knight helicopters. The legend on the sacks about the grain not being sold or exchanged shows a wistful naiveté.

A helicopter demonstrating the capability of rotary-wing craft for use as personnel transports.

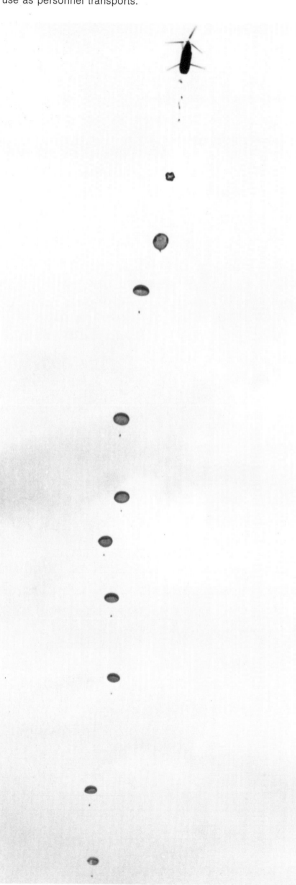

lifted the entire population of 100 children and 50 adults over a 14,000-foot ridge to a relief center.

Conservation organizations increasingly rely on the helicopter to save wildlife. In September 1969, the Los Angeles Animal Regulation Department began airlifting wild animals—captured in populated areas of the rapidly expanding city—to nearby Angeles National Forest. By 1973 Ray Schutte, pilot for the Los Angeles Transportation Bureau, was taking off weekly in a Bell 47G with raccoons, opossums, foxes, owls, and hawks in boxes lashed to the landing skids. Crowded out of their homes by mushrooming suburbs, the animals found a new haven in the federally protected forestlands.

Not all calls to save endangered animals come from conservation groups. Helicopter Combat Support Squadron Two of the U.S. Navy in 22 years had chalked up 1,620 rescues from Greece to Vietnam. On March 29, 1970, Fire Chief Edward Shuhart of Levittown, Pennsylvania, called the helicopter squadron at Lakehurst Naval Air Station in New Jersey. He reported that the day before, William Clarkson and his son Stephen had been horseback riding and had dismounted to walk their horses along a narrow ridge separating two large mud pits. A flock of geese took off, spooking Stephen's horse, Miss Arcadia. She fell 15 feet into the ooze and, in standard horse manner, thrashed about till buried belly-deep. Bulldozer and tractor crews tried all afternoon to rescue the mare, but had given up.

The Soviet Union's aeronautical engineers have kept pace with the West in helicopter design, but their pilots possibly surpass the West's in sheer *chutzpah* as shown in the pictures of a Russian "Hormone" (Ka-25) hovering alongside the aircraft carrier U.S.S. *John F. Kennedy* during maneuvers in the Mediterranean. In the close-up of the Hormone, an antisubmarine helicopter, a Russian photographer crouches in the door to take pictures of American equipment.

An American Sea King from the aircraft carrier U.S.S. *Intrepid* and a Russian "Hormone" from a light cruiser play a dangerous game of "chicken" over the Norwegian Sea in 1971.

Lieutenant Commander Hartley A. Backstrom, responding to the call for help, landed his helicopter on the ridge. Three crewmen put a sling around the mare while a veterinarian gave her a tranquilizing shot. The helicopter lifted the 1,200-pound animal and set her down 800 feet away for the squadron's first rescue of the year.

That winter, in Sweden, a cow moose fell into a lane of crushed ice in the wake of an icebreaker. She had struggled to exhaustion and was near drowning when a Swedish Air Force Boeing HKP-4 came to a hover overhead. Olle Pettersson, the crew chief, tried to lasso the animal, but he lacked the Texas know-how. His crew fabricated a harness from webbing. Olle went down the hoist and slipped the harness over the moose. The helicopter lifted her to land and let her run for several hundred feet with the harness attached to be sure she would not panic and run back into the water. When the crew cut away the harness, the moose disappeared into the forest. She didn't even say good-bye.

From April 11 through April 17, 1970, the world followed with anxiety the trouble-plagued flight of Apollo 13, America's aborted attempt at a third manned lunar landing. During the capsule's third day in space, the service module's oxygen tank exploded, putting in jeopardy the lives of James A. Lovell, Jr., Fred W. Haise, Jr., and John L. Swigert, Jr. When the spacecraft reentered the earth's atmosphere, millions of people clustered before television sets, trying to help the astronauts down safely by sheer willpower. At the announcement that the parachute cluster had come into sight, a guarded sigh of relief swept the world. When the capsule splashed down, though it was five miles from the calculated site, anxious television spectators felt that was close enough for such a hard-luck mission. Five Sikorsky Sea Kings (SH-3As) stood by. Old faithful No. 66, piloted by Comdr. Chuck Smiley, had the astronauts safely aboard the U.S.S. *Iwo Jima* within 45 minutes, to the immense relief of the millions who had agonized through their mission.

On a visit to New York, the Beatles rented a 25-passenger helicopter to take them to their concert on Long Island. The chopper lifted the group to their hotel, bypassing the frenzied fans blockading the entrances.

Perhaps the most closely followed splashdown in spaceflight history was the return of Apollo 13 after a trouble-plagued orbit of the moon. Here the famed Sea King No. 66 hovers over the command module, lowering a Billy Pugh basket to pick up astronauts James A. Lovell, Jr., Fred W. Haise, Jr., and John L. Swigert, Jr., whose possible loss had frightened millions of people when the service module's oxygen tank exploded in outer space. The recovery ship is the U.S.S. *Iwo Jima,* first naval vessel to be built expressly as a helicopter carrier.

A New York City Police Department helicopter patrolling the beaches. The Australian coast guard
is one of several services that patrol swimming areas to warn of sharks.

In the Caribbean Sea on May 2, 1970, a Dutch Antillean Airlines DC-9 ditched 35 miles east of the Virgin Islands. Pan American's Flight 454 heard the Dutch captain's distress signal and began a search. By the time the Pan American plane arrived at the site, the Dutch airliner had sunk, and survivors were clinging to a life raft and the floating escape chute. The PAA pilot guided a U.S. Navy SH-3A helicopter to the scene. Lieutenant Commander James E. Rylee with copilot Lt. (jg.) Donald Hartman and crewmen William Brazzell and Calvin Lindley went first to the chute, for it was a precarious refuge compared to the raft. They picked up 26 persons, the largest number ever hoisted from the sea on a single flight. Rylee flew the heavily loaded craft to the town of Frederiksted on the nearby island of St. Croix. While he was making his round trip, two Coast Guard HH-52A helicopters and a Marine CH-46A arrived from San Juan, Puerto Rico. One of the Coast Guard craft picked up eight survivors, the other rescued four, and the Marine chopper picked up two. The helicopters recovered seven bodies; 16 persons were never found.

After flying unscathed through a combat hitch in Vietnam, a helicopter pilot flying power-line patrol was "shot down" at Denville, New Jersey, with a baseball thrown by a very small boy.

A Bell Long Ranger flies serenely over a traffic jam caused by a minor accident on the highway. Police helicopters patrol main thoroughfares, teaming up with radio stations to alert motorists on driving conditions and traffic bottlenecks, especially during rush hours.

Many police and fire departments operate helicopter ambulance services for quick transfer of accident victims to hospitals.

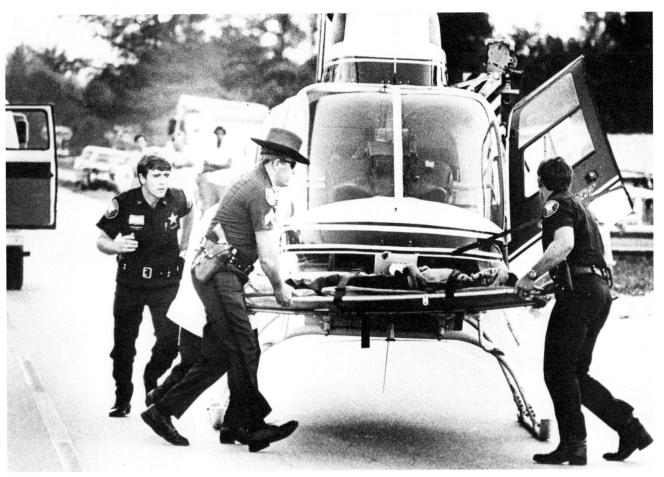

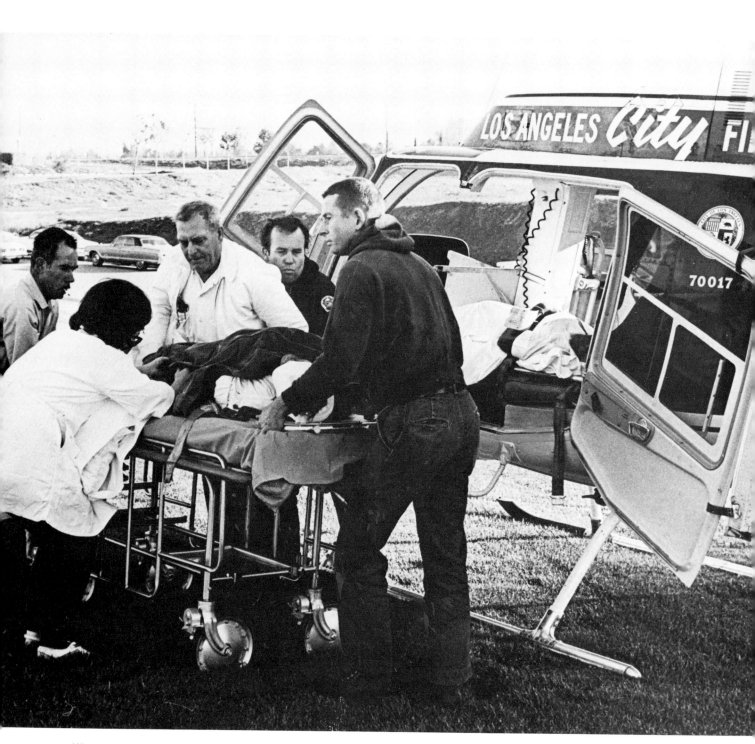

When a major earthquake hit Los Angeles in 1971, several hospitals were among the most severely damaged buildings. The Los Angeles Fire Department, in the forefront of helicopter use in the rescues, is picking up victims for a flight to hospitals still in operation. The machine shown here is a Bell JetRanger.

As the eastern sky lightened on the morning of February 9, 1971, a violent earthquake devastated southern California. For an eternal minute, the ground writhed to a temblor that hit 6.5 on the Richter scale, the worst to hit the state in 38 years. Although centered on the San Fernando Valley, the earthquake spread death and destruction far beyond the valley. The quake killed 64 persons, injured more than 1,000, and did a half-billion-dollars' worth of damage. Overpass bridges dropped to freeways, blocking traffic. Power and telephone lines came down. Traffic and communications came to a standstill.

As it happens, however, Los Angeles is the center of the densest concentration of helicopters in the world.

Within minutes of the earthquake, eight of the Los Angeles Police Department helicopters under Lt. James R. Beall were flying—some over Van Norman Dam, checking to see if the badly damaged structure was going to hold or give way and pour 3.6 billion gallons of water over the homes of 80,000 valley residents. Dam engineers gradually lowered the water level, racing against the threat from the following smaller tremors that threw waves against the weakened earthfill. Other police helicopters flew antilooting patrols.

Lieutenant Claude Cooper of the Los Angeles County Sheriff's Department sent five Bells and two Hughes helicopters to the Olive View Hospital and the almost completely demolished Veterans Hospital, where 48 patients had died. They carried into the devastated area doctors and medical supplies coming in from other parts of the country.

Los Angeles city and county fire department helicopters rescued earthquake victims and carried them to hospitals 50 and 60 miles away. Governor Ronald Reagan flew to the scene in a California Highway Patrol Fairchild-Hiller FH-1100.

Helicopters arrived from other cities, counties, and states and from military and commercial owners. The Bell center at Van Nuys had to be evacuated because of the flood danger from the weakened dam. The Bell helicopters on hand simply flew off on relief errands. The Hughes Tool Company supplied five of its machines. KTLA-TV's JetRanger, equipped for live television coverage, broadcast disaster news and evacuation orders over all three networks and any local station that wanted to lash up. KMPC Radio broadcast warnings from a Bell 47G-4A.

Nobody knows how many helicopters came to the relief of distressed southern California. The sky was so thick with rotary wings within an hour of the quake that Roland Barton, as head of the county's rescue work, preempted airspace under 2,000 feet and required relief craft to get permission from a central location before entering the area.

The dam held. As one pilot said, "Had the dam collapsed, you would have seen helicopters in some *real* action."

The realists who run the Indiana State Police and the Indianapolis Airport Authority maintain a field hospital at the Speedway and keep helicopters standing by during the Indianapolis 500 race. On May 29, 1971, the pace car crashed into portable bleachers filled with photographers, injuring 24 persons. Of the 20 who needed treatment, nine suffered broken arms and legs and internal injuries and required hospitalization. Within minutes four state helicopters carried these accident victims to Indianapolis' Methodist Hospital.

In an experiment to boost reproduction of the threatened whooping crane, conservationists took 14 eggs from nests in Alberta, Canada, and flew them by helicopter to Grays Lake, near Pocatello, Idaho, where they slipped them into nests of greater sandhill cranes. Nine hatched, three were infertile, and two were lost to predators. Of the nine hatched, six survived. The helicopter thus may have helped establish a new flock.

On September 7, 1967, the captain of the Norwegian ferry *Skagerak* decided that Hurricane Faith had abated sufficiently to permit sailing the 80 miles from Kristiansand, Norway, to Hirtshals across Skagerrak Strait in Denmark. With 98 passengers and 47 crewmen aboard, he sailed into the waning storm. Halfway across, a freak wave—"Nothing could have stood against that wave," the captain said—crashed over the stern and poured into the auto hold. Cars went adrift and sloshed about in the 15-foot waves inside the hold. Generators went out and with them the pumps. Danish Air Force Sikorsky S-61s, a Russian trawler, a Norwegian sealer, and a passing freighter rescued all but one small dachshund. Helicopters carried their rescued victims to a beach in Denmark, where ambulances awaited. The *Skagerak* sank next morning.

On August 20, 1942, during World War II, a flight of three U.S. Navy Kingfisher seaplanes was headed for the Aleutian Islands when one slammed into fog-shrouded Mount Buxton in British Columbia. The men aboard walked away, but the plane's wreckage lay on the mountainside for 22 years. On March 12, 1964, two Royal Canadian Air Force Boeing Vertol H-21 helicopters found the plane under four feet of snow. They sling-loaded the hulk to Port Hardy on Vancouver Island for delivery to the Air Museum of Canada. Unable to reassemble the wreckage, the Air Museum gave it to the U.S.S. North Carolina Battleship Commission, for the Kingfisher

had originally been designed to fly observation missions from a battleship or cruiser and would be a welcome addition to the decommissioned vessel being outfitted as a war memorial at Wilmington, North Carolina. Trucks carried the plane's wreckage from Calgary, Alberta, to North Carolina.

The commission had no better luck putting the plane together than the Canadians, so the navy flew the pieces to Texas, where the manufacturer restored it. On June 25, 1971, almost 30 years after it crashed into a Canadian mountain, the plane was dedicated as part of North Carolina's tribute to its warriors.

A Bell JetRanger of the Japanese Maritime Safety Agency in 1974 landed on the hull of a capsized 336-ton oil tanker. A welder cut a hole in the ship's bottom to release trapped sailors.

A Japanese Bell helicopter lifting crewmen from a freighter breaking up in the seas off Japan. Because the beach is close by, the pilot did not hoist the victims aboard but dropped them high and dry on the sand.

To check violations of pollution-control laws, Los Angeles uses a Polaroid color camera, a stopwatch, and a Bell 47G-3B-2A. Patrolling an area of 4,083 square miles, larger than Delaware and Rhode Island put together, the helicopter permits scanning 500 square miles at a time, checking for excessive smoke emissions.

The British pioneered in setting up helicopter search-and-rescue units. Because it is close to busy shipping lanes, the Culdrose Station on the Cornwall coast keeps uncommonly busy. Its routine tasks include lifting stranded hikers from beaches threatened by incoming tides, rescuing mountain climbers who have worked themselves into a corner, picking distressed boaters from stormy seas, plucking injured lighthouse keepers from their towers, and bringing in relief keepers.

Several Culdrose-based helicopters went on a seagoing mission aboard H.M.S. *Eagle* in the South China Sea. On October 7, 1971, the carrier's radio operator intercepted a distress call from the American-owned S.S. *Steel Vendor,* which had been blown onto Loaita reef by Typhoon Elaine. The distressed ship gave its latitude and longitude position and a description of the site. The two did not match by 10 miles and visibility was down to 200 yards, so the carrier launched two Sea Kings, one heading for the latitude-longitude position, the other for the reef. The search spread allowed a radar overlap. Oddly enough, the craft making for the latitude-longitude position picked up the ship first. The pilot lowered a crewman to the deck for a consultation with the ship's captain. The skipper wanted to abandon ship immediately, for already badly holed, it was being smashed against the reef with every surge of the storm-tossed sea.

One Sea King winched up survivors while the other circled overhead as a radio-relay station. After loading 16 sailors, the first Sea King changed places with the second, which picked up 14. Two other helicopters arrived to finish the evacuation. When all had left the ship but the master and the helicopter crewman, the two faced a potentially nasty imbroglio—by tradition, both had to be last to leave the sinking vessel. They solved the dilemma by clinging to the hoist cable together.

A Bell helicopter of Japan's "coast guard" picks up a shipwreck victim from a small freighter, grounded and breaking up in the rising seas. The surface vessel standing by could not approach the distressed craft because of danger of collision.

While not the most violent of hurricanes, Agnes in 1972 caused by far the most costly destruction in North American history as it poured rain on the northeastern states causing floods. The worst damage occurred in Pennsylvania. Helicopters from all the armed services and commercial operators flew hundreds of rescue and supply flights. Here a Sea King from the U.S.S. *Guam* and crewmen in another Sea King search a flooded community for flood victims.

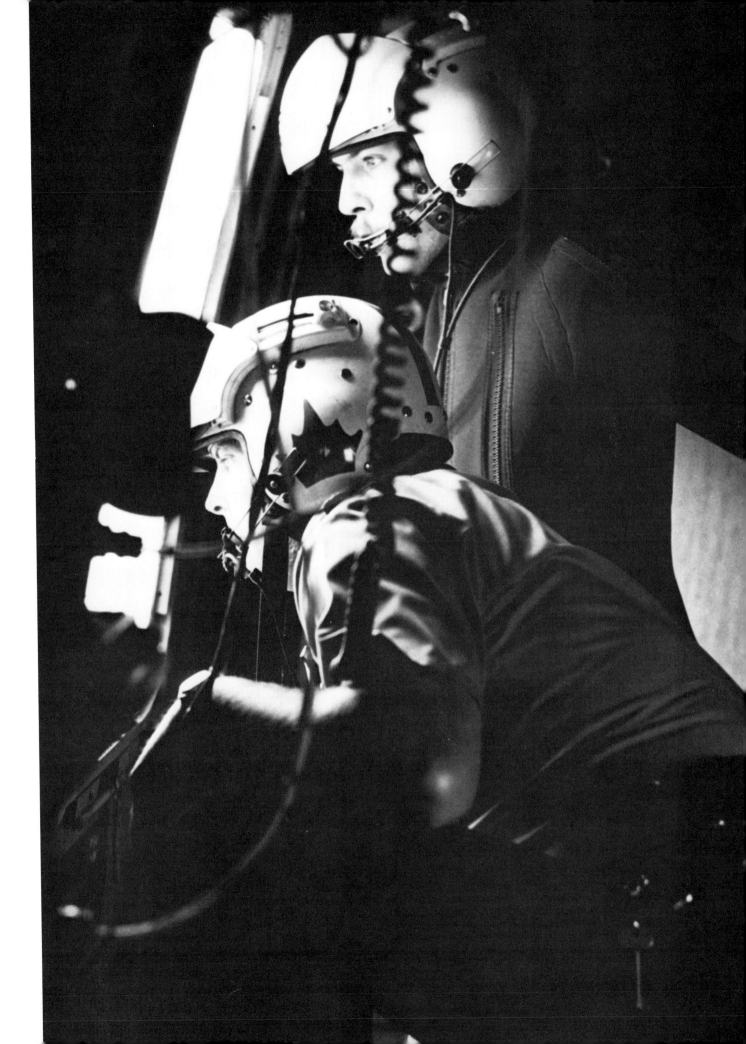

A Chinook carries Red Cross supplies across Wilkes-Barre, Pennsylvania, for victims of Hurricane Agnes.

Left: With characteristic Texas flair, the Dallas police helicopter force puts on a demonstration of formation flying over their happy hunting grounds.

A U.S. Navy helicopter lowers a Billy Pugh basket to pick up a couple stranded on the roof of their house by the floods caused by Hurricane Agnes.

Back in the United States, the helicopter played a savior's role in a totally different kind of situation. Completion of Interstate 5 in March 1972 siphoned off from California Highway 99 most of the long-distance trucking traffic between Los Angeles and San Francisco, threatening to close down Cesare Bianchi's vehicle repair business. Just getting to the interstate highway from his place in Visalia was a 50-mile drive, and reaching the broken-down truck could be another 20 to 50 miles.

Bianchi saved his business—and eventually increased it—by buying a Bell 47G-2 and packing it with lightweight compressors, welding tools, a rip gun, lights, and jacks. He can lift another 750 pounds, which could include spare tires, 55-gallon fuel drums, fuel pumps, and heavy tools. Bianchi gets 15 service calls a month from truckers alone. The mechanic's helicopter is also the only one in the county on standby for rescue work.

In Latin America, a series of high-rise fires anticipated by several years the horror movies of raging infernos. In Mexico City, a fire on Insurgentes Avenue trapped 43 on the roof of an elegant new high rise. Four helicopters from several government services came to their rescue. While three choppers circled, the fourth went into the column of blinding smoke to pick up a maximum load. By taking turns in a spontaneously organized and beautifully coordinated plan, the four small machines rescued the whole party.

The Mexico City fire occurred in 1971. Helicopters saved many more lives in a 1972 high-rise fire in São Paulo, Brazil. The 28-story Pirani Building in the downtown area burst into flame with more than 2,000 shoppers and workers in the department store and offices housed there. Hundreds of persons were injured, many when they jumped from the lower floors. But more than 450 others worked their way to the roof, where 16 helicopters flew through flames for six hours to lift them to safety. Eighteen persons died in the fire, several jumping to their deaths.

Chicago Fire Commissioner Robert J. Quinn, one of the world's foremost exponents of helicopter use, demonstrated to the National Fire Protection Association a method of fighting high-rise fires by sending aloft a one-inch high-pressure hose rigged to a boom projecting from a Bell JetRanger. The demonstration worked on a simulated fire 26 stories high, and later it succeeded at 40 stories. Commissioner Quinn said the method would work at 50 or 60 stories.

On July 23, 1973, Capt. Alberto Guingue Ossa, who heads Colombia's largest commercial helicopter operation, while driving to work, noticed smoke pouring from the 40-story Avianca Building in downtown Bogotá.

"At that instant I remembered reading in a magazine about the case of the aerial action carried out by a fleet of helicopters when there was a fire in a 28-story building in São Paulo, Brazil. . . . I thought that being a helicopter pilot, I could be useful if they let me."

Captain Ossa commandeered a motorcycle policeman to clear a path for him to the airport.

"When we arrived at the airport, two mechanics were already waiting for me, and the helicopter was ready to fly." He took the two mechanics along to help control the crowd on the roof.

"When we neared the building, smoke was beginning to impede visibility. This was the time to fly around the tower, and with a megaphone,

A Bell UH-1N on a rescue mission around a towering inferno in South America. Brazil now requires all buildings higher than a fire ladder can reach to maintain a helistop on the roof.

When the Avianca Building caught fire in Bogotá, Colombia, a helicopter pilot raced to the scene and landed mechanics on the roof to organize an orderly evacuation. By radio he arranged with police to close off a nearby plaza as a landing field and with medical authorities to send ambulances and a field treatment team.

we tried to control the nerves and the panic that were beginning to affect the people on the roof."

Smoke hampered the landing, and the pilot worried about a wall that obstructed his approach. After landing, his mechanics had to keep the crowd from trying to board all at once. The mechanics organized a priority system, evacuating first the aged, women, and children.

"About 200 people were waiting to be rescued. In order . . . to calm them, the two mechanics who accompanied me stayed with them on the roof and attended to the most urgent cases, while I made the first flight."

The pilot picked Bolivar Plaza as a convenient landing site and by radio asked police to rope it off and to send medical help. By his second landing, medical teams were waiting. Other helicopters arrived to help with the evacuation. When all the victims were down, helicopters carried police, firemen, doctors, and civil-defense workers back to the roof to search the upper floors for trapped victims.

Four persons died in the fire, and another 63 suffered burns. The death toll would have been staggering had it not been for the helicopter's rooftop rescue, for the blaze started on the 14th floor and spread quickly, sealing off escape for all those on the 26 floors above.

Less fortunate were the hundreds of persons in the 25-story Joelma Building in São Paulo, Brazil, when the brand-new structure burst into flame on February 1, 1974. A dozen helicopters from various agencies tried to rescue survivors on the roof, but projections and structural weaknesses made landings impossible. Major Sergio Pradatski of the Brazilian Air Force put the skids of his UH-1H against the parapet and hovered while victims—huddled between gaps in the roof—shinnied across. A rotor clipped a projecting wall, but Pradatski continued to carry victims to the street; he rescued between 80 and 100—nobody kept count. Well over 200 persons died in the Joelma fire as compared with the 18 who died in a potentially worse disaster at the Pirani Building

Rustlers regularly spirit away butchered cattle and hogs by helicopter. Poachers decimated alligator populations by spotting them from the air and descending for a quick kill, then escaping by air from game wardens. They overdid it, for the alligator is now on the endangered species list.

two years earlier. The difference was the ability of helicopters to land on the Pirani roof. Brazilian law now requires all buildings more than 15 floors high to have helicopter landing pads on the roof. Los Angeles has followed suit. The helicopter-conscious Chicago Fire Department is surveying every high-rise rooftop for its availability as a landing site.

At Timikia, in New Guinea, while under contract to the Freeport Sulphur Company, another Louisiana firm, a PHI helicopter assembled in the jungle attracted a crowd of primitive natives to witness the maiden flight. When the engine fired up with a roar, the frightened spectators scattered into the jungle. One woman who had been nursing a baby and carrying a piglet under one arm dropped both and disappeared into the foliage. A few seconds passed, and she recovered enough courage to dash out and grab up . . . . . the pig.

During the wintery month of March 1973, thousands of people daily braved the weather in Toronto, Canada, to watch a Sikorsky Skycrane nicknamed Olga lift components to build a 335-foot spire atop the CN Tower. Newspapers published daily timetables of the scheduled helicopter lifts, and television stations broadcast bulletins

Igor Sikorsky died on October 26, 1972, full of years and honors.

The U.S. Navy pioneered in refueling at sea,
thus extending its range of action enormously.
The helicopter has added a new service—
transporting materials too heavy for
conventional transfer methods at sea.

Vertical reprovisioning at sea. Two Sea Knights
lift supplies from fleet oilers and replenishment
ships while a third flies in for another load, all
bound for assault vessels short distances away.

A Chinook of the Canadian Forces delivers a 5,700-pound piece of a statue called "Love—L'Amour" 60 miles, from Renfrew, Ontario, to Hull, Quebec.

Increased use of camper huts in White Mountain National Forest created a sanitation problem. The Appalachian Mountain Club built outhouses (a helicopter hauled the material to the mountaintop) and installed containerized toilets. A Bell 47G-3B-2 honey wagon lifts them out for emptying and replacement.

announcing cancellations or changes. City officials had to set aside a spectator area.

The Skycrane began working near the 1,500-foot level by bringing down a 47-ton crane in seven lifts. During a 26-day span, the Skycrane made 55 flights, most of them to lift pre-assembled seven-ton sections of the antenna that was to top the tower. The last six sections were held in place by the giant helicopter while the lone steeplejack, Paul Mitchell, a structural-steel foreman, bolted them in place. He stayed in contact with the pilot by radio.

When the Skycrane set in place the last segment, the CN Tower, standing 1,815 feet high, took its place in the Guinness bible for settling bar arguments as the world's tallest free-standing structure. Pilots Larry Pravcek, Rip Green, and Dave Kohornen and mechanics Larry Hough and Charlie Hushbeck were local celebrities during the tower job, a rare sensation for them because most of the time they were lifting logs for Erickson Air Crane of Medford, Oregon, deep in the forest and far from admiring crowds.

A Bell 205A-1 lifting in sections of a transmission tower for bringing power from the Churchill Falls Project in Canada's subarctic to the populated areas of the south.

Helicopters have added a new dimension to logging in the Pacific Northwest by lifting logs from the cutting site to yarding sites, thus eliminating the damage to forest floor caused by conventional methods of dragging in the timber by cable. The craft shown here is one of a fleet of Boeing Vertol 107s used by Columbia Helicopters of Oregon in its logging operations.

Pilot Don Hanson of Petroleum Helicopters, flying supply missions to the Ertsberg Copper Mine in Irian Jaya, Indonesia, on the island of New Guinea, encountered a strange mixture of savage competitiveness and communal generosity. After landing at the village of Kokonau, he scattered candy among the children gathered to witness his arrival. They battled ferociously to grab as much as possible, then shared with the losers to be sure everybody had an equal cut.

Logging with heavy-lift helicopters to bring the timber out from terrain inaccessible to conventional tractor and highline tower methods had begun on an experimental basis in the Pacific Northwest in 1971. Attempts in Austria, Scotland, and the Soviet Union in the 1950s had faltered because the craft used could not lift enough low-cost logs to turn a profit. With rising timber prices and more powerful machines available, however, Jack Erickson, president of Erickson Lumber Company in Marysville, California, and Wes Lematta, president of Columbia Helicopters, Incorporated, in Portland, Oregon, tried helicopter logging again.

Using a Skycrane with a 20,000-pound lift capability in Plumas National Forest and Siskiyou National Forest, Erickson and Lematta demonstrated that the time had come for helicopter logging. The project's success led to the formation of Erickson Air Crane. Columbia Helicopters, which maintains a fleet of Boeing Vertol 107s with an 11,500-pound sling capability, has become a major helicopter logger.

To handle contracts with tight deadlines, Lematta developed a technique for night logging. A typical job that could not have been done by conventional methods was lifting a large stand of timber blown down by a storm and in danger of being lost to insects and rot. Pilots of Columbia's

In Peru an American helicopter, a Chinook, demonstrates its value as a salvage tool by bringing in the carcass of a wrecked Canberra bomber.

Boeing Vertols—which once flew for New York Airways from the Pan American Building roof to the airports—located themselves by lights on 30-foot towers spotted in the forest at yarding and loading sites. The helicopters carried 12 to 14 floodlights, and the loggers wore fluorescent vests and headlamps on their helmets. The lumberjacks made up a load, or "turn," of one to nine felled logs lashed by a ½-inch choker to the helicopter's fixed cable for a lift to the yarding area.

At first loggers resisted night operations, but they discovered its advantages—lower temperatures and fewer insects.

At Gifford Pinchot National Forest in Washington, Boeing Vertols raced a deadline to pluck out 21.7 million board feet of Douglas fir infested with the bark beetle. The timber had to come out before May 1, 1975, to prevent spread of the infestation.

Although helicopter logging was not developed as an environmental tool, protection of the forest is an important side benefit. By lifting logs straight up and carrying them through the air to the yard, choppers prevent scouring of the forest floor by churning tractor treads and thrashing logs dragged by cable.

The heavy-lift Sea Stallion hauling a Bronco over the Patuxent River in Maryland. The Bronco is an experimental vertical short takeoff and landing (VSTOL) craft of a type that one day may replace or at least complement helicopter service.

Inspired by a movie, Irish terrorists hijacked an Irish Helicopters' Alouette and forced the pilot, Thompson Boyes, to land in the exercise yard at Mountjoy Prison, in Dublin. They took out three top-security prisoners, members of the Irish Republican Army, and abandoned the chopper on Baldoyle Race Course, five miles away. Several months later, terrorists hijacked a Bo-105 of Irish Helicopters and made a bombing run on a police station on the Ulster border.

On July 5, 1974, the Search and Rescue crew on watch at Whidbey Island Naval Air Station in Washington got a call from the Whatcom County Sheriff's Office asking for help to rescue a young woman who had hurt herself badly in a fall on a 40-degree snow-covered mountain slope near New-halem. At the site, Lawrence A. Gallwas, three volunteer climbers, and a Stokes litter were lowered 50 feet to a small outcropping. Gallwas' report follows:

"Upon reaching the victim, I checked her for serious bleeding. Most bleeding had almost stopped, but the area showed signs of profuse bleeding earlier.... During the examination, I discovered her left leg (femur) was broken and she had a broken back. She had no feeling in her lower body, but there was a pulse and heat in her legs. She could move both arms and turn her head. She was bleeding slightly from both ears and had massive bruised areas around her trunk. One or more ribs were broken, and she had difficulty breathing.

"The Stokes litter was placed on a hollowed-out area below her, and the four of us then moved her to it after I briefed the other three. Ice axes were staked at the Stokes and at my feet to prevent anything from slipping on the wet snow. Once she was in the Stokes, I asked her if she had any unusual pain or felt anything [bones]

move when we moved her. She answered no.

"I motioned for the helo to move in and pick us up. As she left the ground, she lost consciousness, stopped breathing, and I could no longer feel a pulse or heartbeat. Three times she was lowered back to the snow, while I administered mouth-to-mouth and external heart massage. Each time she seemed to panic as she was raised. I realized the shock was getting worse and got her breathing in good rhythm with a weak but steady pulse, hooked the Stokes to the hoist, and sent her up. I immediately signaled the helo of her condition and waved them off as the minute or two needed to hoist me would probably jeopardize the woman's life. [She made a complete recovery.]

"Clouds appeared to be moving lower, and I

A Sea King delivers mail to the nuclear-powered submarine *Skate*, a morale booster for men who may be at sea for months at a time.

Probably the most important commercial use of helicopters is the servicing of offshore oil rigs. The largest operator is Petroleum Helicopters of Louisiana, which employs more than 500 pilots. Sikorsky S-61Ns fly in relief crews, supplies, and tools and fly out off-duty workmen and the occasional casualty.

decided to hike out with the three climbers. We followed the only possible route to Newhalem, which was an almost vertical climb to the top and then over a couple of ice fields. Not knowing if the helo would be able to get back into the area, I felt, and still feel, the hike out was warranted."

By far the largest commercial operator of helicopters in the world is Petroleum Helicopters, Incorporated. (Because it was founded as Petroleum Bell Helicopters, old-timers in the oil fields still call the company "Pet Bell.") In 1976 the corporation operated some 240 helicopters and employed more than 500 pilots. It has logged over two million hours of rotary-wing flight time in half the countries of the world.

In the middle of the night, a Royal Swedish Air Force HKP-4 helicopter made a run to the cruise ship Svea Regina in the Baltic Sea to pick up a woman suffering labor pains every five minutes. By the time the chopper circled the afterdeck, intervals were down to three minutes. Hundreds of passengers witnessed the lift of the woman and her husband. Two hours later, the woman gave birth to a girl in a normal delivery. The baby's premature arrival spoiled the couple's honeymoon cruise, given to them as a wedding present.

PHI has recorded many firsts—landing a passenger on Mount Whitney and the midair catch of a NASA suborbital rocket payload among them. During Hurricane Donna, PHI machines rescued 216 Puerto Ricans from trees and roofs.

By the mid-1970s, helicopters had found more than a hundred uses. Most of these were routine applications, such as agricultural spraying, cattle ranching, drying rain-soaked athletic fields, mapping, and political campaigning (Mrs. Philip Hart piloted the helicopter flying her husband about Michigan during his race for the Senate). Some uses were more exotic; for example, transporting Santa Claus to orphanages and supermarkets, towing water-skiers, smuggling and chasing smugglers, and spray-painting the balls suspended on power lines to warn off low-flying aircraft.

After Egypt agreed to reopen the Suez Canal as part of a peace settlement with Israel, the U.S. Navy joined the international effort to clear the watercourse of mines and sunken vessels. Here a Sea Stallion in April 1974 tows a magnetic minesweeper to detonate with impunity explosives lying on the canal bed.

7

What's Next?

The mother of invention and man's ingenuity seemingly have pressed the helicopter into virtually every conceivable service. A few services still remain undeveloped, however, especially those demanding bigger aircraft.

Before his death, Sikorsky reported that technology already existed for a 70-ton lift capacity, or possibly even a 100-ton lift. (The present Sky-crane can lift 10 tons with ease.) The 70-ton lift could transport the 65-ton battle tanks of an armored division across rivers, swamps, and enemy ambushes. Minefields and tank traps would no longer block swift deployment of armor.

In Central and South America, the mahogany tree has the curious habit of growing alone, a long distance across the jungle from the next one, making conventional logging impossibly expensive. Heavy-lift helicopters could pluck a fortune in mahogany from impenetrable jungles.

Skycranes could help establish a new industry of prefabricated houses built wider than now possible because the choppers could lift the sections over narrow bridges and highways.

Growing sea trade is choking harbors at newly rich oil-exporting countries. Some freighters have to stand off the Nigerian coast for months waiting for dock space. Aboard one Japanese vessel, stalled for almost a year, the crew ran out of water and food. Existing Chinooks and Sky-cranes could unplug those bottlenecks by air-

lightering from offshore anchorages directly to warehouses ashore. The capability was clearly demonstrated by the U.S. Army in Vietnam.

Britain's Royal Navy is going all out for helicopters—phasing out fixed-wing aircraft carriers, shifting emphasis to what it calls "commando ships" (helicopter carriers), and fitting all other vessels from frigate size on up with helicopter landing pads.

The most urgent and obvious use of all is seriously underdeveloped, however, because the industry will not make commercially the big passenger craft already in existence for military use. Short-haul helicopter passenger service from city center to city center—the Boston-New York-Phila-delphia-Baltimore-Washington corridor, for example, or the Paris-London cross-Channel jump—would save hours now wasted riding traffic-choked highways to airports far from downtown areas.

Operating costs of rotary-wing craft run roughly three times those of fixed-wing craft of the same capacity. Each rotary-wing passenger flight, therefore, must carry enough travelers to absorb the large costs. Sabena's experiment at intercity travel in Western Europe failed because the largest craft they flew, the S-58, had an insufficient capacity for a payload.

"Had Sabena waited for the S-61," according to Jock Cameron, the head of British Airways' highly successful helicopter services, "they would have survived. That's why the helicopter service between Naples and Capri failed."

Himself a famed pioneer helicopter pilot, Cameron is a fervent and florid orator on the virtues and future of vertical flight.

"The S-61 we use on the Isles of Scilly scheduled passenger flights does fine for that short jump. It has boosted traffic from 8,000 annually in fixed-wing craft to 80,000 in rotary-wing craft. More than 98 percent of takeoffs and landings are precisely on schedule. Most important, the line makes a tidy profit.

"For the Paris-London flight, we would have to have a bigger plane. The Sikorsky S-65, a civilian 44-passenger version of the CH-53, would be ideal—and Sikorsky, after all, has built 350 of them for the military. But Sikorsky won't build the civilian version.

"The next jump forward in transportation has to be the city center to city center flight. Take the Paris-London run. We were doing it with fixed-wing in 3½ hours in 1930. Now it takes four hours. With an S-65, you could leave Battersea in the heart of London and be at Issy-les-Moulineaux in southwest Paris in 1½ hours. The ironic thing is that the supposedly cheaper-to-operate fixed-

Heavy-lift helicopters already available could open harborless countries to sea commerce or unblock ports in newly oil-rich countries such as Nigeria by lightering containers or sling loads from offshore freighters directly to warehouses or railroad sidings. The heavy-lift helicopter's ability to speed freight movement from ship to shore has already been demonstrated in Iran.

Commercial helicopter operators around the world are waiting on Sikorsky to put into production the S-65 (civilian version of the CH-53 Sea Stallion), shown here flying over Hartford, Connecticut. Jock Cameron, chief of helicopter operations for British Airways, has predicted that availability of the S-65 would revolutionize short-haul air traffic, making intercity flight profitable overnight.

As the search for oil moves farther and farther out on the continental shelf around the world, the demand for the Sikorsky S-65 becomes more urgent. Civilian certification would cost about $23 million, however, and the Sikorsky company is understandably waiting for enough orders to justify the expense.

One of the most promising of the craft adaptable for passenger service from city center to city center was the Faery Rotodyne that combined the helicopter lift principle with propeller drive for forward flight. Lack of interest by the military caused the Kaman company to drop plans for further development.

The most frustrating of failures for the advocates of city-center-to-city-center flight was the cancellation by the U.S. military of Boeing Vertol's experimental heavy-lift helicopter when it was already 94 percent completed. The carcass waits in a hangar for the U.S. Congress to come to its senses and authorize resumption of its development. The craft would carry up to 110 passengers and would make intercity travel by helicopter eminently profitable.

wing craft cannot make a profit on a 200-mile trip, but the more expensive rotary-wing craft can. By charging first-class fares (the savings on limousines and taxis would more than make up the extra charge over tourist-class fare), British Airways could make money with a 50-percent load.

"As for safety, there is no comparison. A properly maintained helicopter is much safer than any 747. It scares me to roar down a runway at 160 knots just to get airborne. A century from now, people will look back on the fixed-wing age and marvel at the reckless courage of crews and passengers."

Officials of Sikorsky Aircraft, a division of United Technologies Corporation (formerly United

Aircraft), said they could not be sure of enough orders for the S-65 model to justify the estimated $23 million cost of getting FAA (Federal Aviation Administration) certification for civilian use. Jock Cameron countered with the argument that helicopters need a tiny fraction of the airport space and runway construction required by conventional craft and that the difference in cost would be well spent by government subsidizing development of suitable intercity machines.

Even more frustrating than the nonavailability of the S-65 is the cancellation by the U.S. government of Boeing Vertol's experimental heavy-lift machine after spending $188 million on it and stopping $14 million short of completing the job.

As innovative as the great lifting power of the Sikorsky Skycrane —up to 10 tons—is the pod concept. The Skycrane configuration makes possible lifting truck container bodies, mobile hospital pods, passenger vans, and other modular units for swift and traffic-free delivery over long distances.

The 94-percent-completed machine now standing idle in a hangar would have carried up to 110 passengers on intercity center flights, five times the load that Jock Cameron said would make money on the Paris-London haul.

Even a vertical flight from city center to airport for boarding conventional craft would save hours. The Grand Old Man, Sikorsky, who had an uncanny ability to see far into the future, in 1964 outlined one method of swift delivery of passengers from city centers to conventional aircraft at outlying airports.

"Communication between city helicopters and airplane terminals may be better achieved by the use of a crane with a pod than with a cabin helicopter. The advantages of such an arrangement are as follows. Today aircraft parking space is already at a premium, even at air terminals, and this same fact would hold true to a far greater extent for centrally located city heliports. Loading and unloading of, say, 50 passengers or, in the near future, 100 passengers with their luggage would take several minutes with a cabin helicopter. On the other hand, disconnecting a pod from a crane helicopter would take less than one minute, and approximately 12 pods could be parked in a space that would be required to park a single aircraft of similar lifting capacity. Furthermore, when a pod is flown to a heliport, it could immediately be lowered by platform elevator or otherwise moved into a passenger lounge or moved or towed to a location where loading and unloading of passengers and luggage could be taken care of with greater convenience, thus freeing precious space on the landing platform."

The convenience of flying over traffic is not the only argument for helicopter passenger service. Few modes of transport, not even the luxury cruise ship or crack train, give the passenger so delightful an experience as a low-level cross-country helicopter run. It is the ideal sight-seeing vehicle.

The flight from Penzance in Cornwall to the Isles of Scilly 25 miles offshore, now the only

Two experimental vertical-lift machines built by Hiller Helicopters (now Hiller Aircraft). The rotary-wing craft is the U.S. Marines' XROE-1 Rotorcycle. The flying disk (the rotor is at the bottom of the disk) is controlled in horizontal flight by shifting the weight of the pilot.

The possibilities of a Buck Rogers type, personal vertical-lift gimmick has fascinated designers from the beginning of vertical flight. This rocket device is a product of Bell designers. The device flew successfully around a 300-foot elliptical course and looks like lots of fun, but it has not been put into production.

paying scheduled passenger service in the world, takes the traveler over the lush Cornish country-side low enough to look into the gardens of country manors, count the standing slabs in a small version of Stonehenge left by prehistoric man, fly excitingly close to the surf-lashed cliffs at Land's End, wave at sailors on trawlers resting under the lee of the islands, and settle gently onto the tiny landing pad—all the space the islands can spare from their fields of winter-blooming flowers.

One flight from Penzance to the Isles of Scilly is enough to convert the most blasé traveler from all other vehicles to the helicopter.

Index